HUMAN
PRIDE

HUMAN PRIDE

OPTIMIZING YOUR HUMAN POTENTIAL IN A DIGITAL JOB MARKET

RON THURSTON

LIONCREST
PUBLISHING

HUMAN PRIDE

Optimizing Your Human Potential in a Digital Job Market

FIRST EDITION

ISBN 978-1-5445-4829-6 Paperback
     978-1-5445-4830-2 Ebook

To My Husband

You remind me every day that true strength comes from
embracing who we are and celebrating it fully—
the ultimate expression of human pride.
Your faith in me and your steady presence are
the foundation of everything I do.

I am endlessly grateful to share this
extraordinary adventure with you—
whether navigating nature's vast landscapes
or finding joy in the smallest of spaces.

I love you.

CONTENTS

INTRODUCTION

SETTING THE STAGE FOR HUMAN PRIDE

A Journey to Self-Acceptance, Empathy, and Empowerment in Your Career

Pause for a moment. Take a deep breath. Think about the extraordinary journey that's led you to this point. Reflect on the experiences, challenges, triumphs, and dreams that have shaped you into the person you are today. Each of those moments, no matter how big or small, has contributed to a unique blend of wisdom, resilience, and potential that only you carry. Now, absorb this truth: you are invaluable, not just because of what you do but because of who you are.

By choosing to read this book, you've made a powerful decision. You've chosen yourself—your potential, your humanity, and your future. I'm deeply grateful to be part of this journey with you.

By choosing to read this book, you've made a powerful decision. You've chosen yourself—your potential, your humanity, and your future. I'm deeply grateful to be part of this journey with you.

1

This book is more than a guide to career success; it's a call to action to reclaim the essence of what makes us human in a world dominated by technological change. It's about tapping into the power of **human pride**—the unwavering belief in your inherent value—to foster authentic relationships, ignite creativity, and inspire purposeful leadership.

WHY HUMAN PRIDE MATTERS

Human pride isn't about boasting or seeking external validation. It's a quiet, transformative force rooted in self-respect and the acknowledgment of your worth. It's about embracing the entirety of your journey—both your achievements and setbacks—and seeing them as vital parts of your growth.

> **Human pride isn't about boasting or seeking external validation. It's a quiet, transformative force rooted in self-respect and the acknowledgment of your worth.**

When you embrace this mindset, you unlock a wellspring of **authenticity** and **empathy**. You see yourself as an integral part of the human tapestry, where every thread, every person, and every story add richness and strength. This shift empowers you to lead with intention, collaborate with openness, and create with passion.

In a world where technology often overshadows personal connection, human pride becomes our necessary counterbalance. It reminds us that our most profound contributions—our creativity, curiosity, and empathy—are irreplaceable. These qualities define our humanity, enabling us to thrive in ways no algorithm or automation ever could.

WHY NOW?

The idea for this book was born from my experience writing and sharing *Retail Pride: The Guide to Celebrating Your Accidental Career.* Published in October 2020, *Retail Pride* quickly became a bestseller, resonating deeply with those in retail and beyond. It shared a simple yet powerful truth: "The most important person in any company is the one standing in front of the customer."

In a world where technology often overshadows personal connection, human pride becomes our necessary counterbalance.

In *Retail Pride*, I highlighted the often-overlooked value of human connection in shaping experiences. A genuine smile, a thoughtful question, or a moment of undivided attention—these actions build trust, loyalty, and community. No marketing campaign or technology can replicate the impact of these authentic interactions.

The response was overwhelming. People shared how the book validated their experiences, reignited their passion, and helped them see their roles as essential. The principles of human pride extend far beyond retail—they are universal.

As the world navigates rapid technological advancement and shifting workplace dynamics, the need to celebrate our shared humanity has never been greater. It's easy to feel lost in the noise of automation, metrics, and digital transformation. But this is precisely why human pride is so timely. It's a reminder that our humanity—our ability to connect, empathize, and inspire—remains our greatest strength.

MY WHY

This book's genesis transcended the immediate moment; it was deeply personal. Over decades of leadership, I've witnessed the transformative power of pride in action. I've seen recognition illuminate employees, shared purpose uniting teams, and valued employees surpass expectations.

Reflecting on my early career, I remember the profound impact of leaders who celebrated my growth and potential. Their belief in me fueled my confidence and shaped my leadership philosophy. I wanted to pay it forward, creating environments where people felt proud of their work and were empowered to thrive.

In one of my most recent roles as a vice president of retail, I scaled this philosophy. I inherited teams struggling with low morale and high turnover, but I saw an opportunity to rebuild trust and ignite pride. By listening with intention, recognizing contributions, and fostering collaboration, we transformed the culture into one of engagement, innovation, and record-breaking success.

During those moments when I stood with a team refocused on its purpose, I witnessed the limitless potential of human pride.

A MOMENT OF REFLECTION

Before we dive deeper, let's pause for a moment of gratitude and reflection. This practice will ground you, celebrate your uniqueness, and prepare your heart for the journey ahead:

> ▶ **What experiences have shaped your sense of pride?** Reflect on the moments that defined your journey. How have they influenced the way you see yourself and your contributions?

- ▶ **How do you bring humanity to your work?** Think about how you connect with others in your personal and professional life. What unique qualities make your presence impactful?
- ▶ **What legacy do you want to create?** Consider the mark you want to leave on your team, your community, and the world. What drives you to keep striving?

THE JOURNEY AHEAD

This book is an invitation to rediscover the power of your humanity in a world that often prioritizes technology over connection. Together, we'll explore actionable strategies to lead with authenticity, foster meaningful relationships, and unlock the untapped potential within you and those around you.

Through the lens of human pride, you'll learn to harness your unique strengths, embrace your story, and inspire transformative change in your life and work. Most importantly, you'll gain the tools to build a culture of pride and connection wherever you go, leaving a legacy of purpose and impact.

Thank you for choosing this book, for choosing growth, and for choosing yourself. Let's embark on this journey together and unlock the extraordinary power of human pride to create a future filled with connection, innovation, and success.

This is your moment.

With gratitude and love,

Ron

PART 1

FOR THE JOB SEEKER

Your Career,
Your Legacy:
Navigating with
Purpose and Pride

Human pride isn't about boasting or seeking external validation. It's a quiet, transformative force rooted in self-respect and the acknowledgment of your worth.

CHAPTER 1

STANDING OUT IN THE AGE OF AI

Your Blueprint for Success

Stepping into today's job market feels like navigating a thrilling, yet uncertain, frontier. **Artificial intelligence (AI)** has revolutionized how employers seek talent, introducing empowering and ntimidating tools. If you've ever feared that an algorithm could eclipse your unique talents, or a machine might reject you before you've had the chance to shine, you're not alone.

To ignite your confidence, no algorithm can replicate your humanity. Your creativity, emotional intelligence, and ability to forge meaningful connections remain unmatched. These qualities fuel innovation, nurture collaboration, and inspire teams to thrive. Employers aren't just searching for candidates who can keep up with technology. They're seeking those who can infuse it with heart, intuition, and originality.

Your ability to learn and use new technology shows how adaptable and positive you are. Engaging with AI-driven hiring platforms isn't about surviving the process; it's about showcasing your

> **You are more than a resume. Your story, experiences, and determination transcend keywords and algorithms. You bring a voice and presence that no machine can replicate.**

forward-thinking approach and readiness to lead in a rapidly evolving world. Every step—whether navigating applicant tracking systems or leveraging digital platforms—is an opportunity to unleash your ingenuity and highlight your unique character.

You are more than a resume. Your story, experiences, and determination transcend keywords and algorithms. You bring a voice and presence that no machine can replicate. This chapter will guide you in harnessing these human traits, integrating them with technological savvy, and positioning yourself as an invaluable asset in today's job market.

WHY TRUST ME ON THIS JOURNEY?

You might wonder, "Why should I trust these strategies?" Let me share a piece of my story. With over thirty-five years in retail leadership, I've walked in your shoes—hiring, mentoring, and building teams for some of the world's most iconic brands. From managing individual stores to overseeing hundreds of locations as a vice president, I've witnessed how human pride, resilience, and **adaptability** can transform not just careers but entire workplace cultures.

Today, as co-founder of a retail recruiting company, I collaborate with candidates and businesses to navigate the hiring process in this new era. I help people craft standout resumes, refine their interview skills, and present their most authentic selves. My insights have come from decades at the intersection of human connection and technology. What I offer isn't just theory—it's a practical, actionable guide built on real-world lessons.

Your journey is yours, but you don't have to navigate it alone. Together, we'll unlock your potential, amplify your human edge, and embrace the opportunities that await.

A MOMENT OF REFLECTION

Before diving into strategies and tools, let's take a moment to reflect. These questions will help you reconnect with your strengths, values, and story—elements that will set you apart:

1. **When has your creativity or empathy made a meaningful impact?** Reflect on a situation where your actions sparked change or connection. How did this experience shape your understanding of your abilities?
2. **What technological tools or skills have you adopted?** Consider how these innovations enhance your ability to showcase value in a job market shaped by AI.
3. **How have you shown resilience?** Think about challenges you've overcome in your career or personal life. What lessons did you learn that highlight your adaptability and determination?

As you ponder these questions, remember, you aren't competing with technology; you're complementing it. Your story, creativity, and human edge make you irreplaceable. Let's embark on this journey together, grounded in the belief that your potential is limitless and your impact immeasurable.

Onward we go!

STRATEGIES FOR THE MODERN JOB SEEKER

I've created five strategies to help you excel in a digital world.

Strategy One. Demystify Applicant Tracking Systems by Crafting a Resume That Gets Noticed

Navigating online job applications through platforms like LinkedIn or Indeed often means encountering **applicant tracking systems (ATSs)**. These digital gatekeepers scan resumes to streamline hiring, but your application may feel like a barrier if it isn't tailored to meet their criteria.

Picture this: you're the perfect candidate with all the qualifications, yet your resume doesn't reach human hands because it fails the ATS screening. It's a disheartening situation, but the fix is simpler than you think. Optimizing your resume for ATSs ensures your application not only clears the system but also shines for hiring managers.

> **While a generic resume might save time, a customized application showcases your attention to detail, dedication, and understanding of the position's unique demands.**

In today's competitive job market, a tailored resume is your secret weapon. The bespoke outfit must fit the role precisely. While a generic resume might save time, a customized application showcases your attention to detail, dedication, and understanding of the position's unique demands.

Here are five elements to help your resume breeze past ATS filters and captivate hiring managers.

1. Targeted Keyword Integration

Keywords are the language ATSs understand best. Review the job description to identify core skills and requirements, then seamlessly incorporate these terms into your resume.

Pro Tip: Use tools like ChatGPT to extract frequently mentioned keywords from the job posting. Weave these phrases naturally into your descriptions of roles, achievements, and skills.

Why It Works: Aligning your resume with the job description's language ensures it resonates with both ATS algorithms and hiring managers, spotlighting you as a candidate who truly understands the role.

2. Use Standard Headings and Job Titles

While creativity can elevate your brand, resume structure isn't the place for experimentation. Use universally recognized section headers like "Work Experience," "Education," and "Skills." Avoid unconventional titles that could confuse ATSs.

Why It Matters: Simplicity and consistency make your resume accessible to both ATSs and human reviewers, preventing them from overlooking critical qualifications.

3. Embrace Minimalist Formatting

Elaborate designs, unusual fonts, or graphics might catch a human eye but can trip up an ATS. Opt for clean layouts that prioritize clarity and readability.

Best Practices: Use standard fonts like Arial or Times New Roman. Avoid tables, images, or symbols that ATSs might misinterpret. Structure achievements and responsibilities with bullet points.

Why It Matters: A straightforward format ensures your resume is both ATS-friendly and visually appealing to hiring managers.

4. Tailor Each Application

Every role is unique, and your resume should reflect that. Customize your content to highlight the experiences and skills most relevant to the job.

Why It Matters: A tailored resume shows genuine interest in the position and helps establish a strong connection with hiring managers, increasing your chances of an interview invitation.

5. Highlight Relevant Skills with Impact

Your resume should showcase a balance of technical expertise and interpersonal abilities. Use the job description as a guide to prioritize both hard and soft skills.

Actionable Tip: Instead of listing skills, provide context. For example, write, "Developed an innovative workflow that reduced project timelines by 20 percent" instead of simply stating "problem-solving."

Why It Works: Quantifying achievements makes your skills more compelling and memorable.

Now that you're armed with these strategies, it's time to refine your resume. Carefully analyze job descriptions, integrate relevant keywords, and focus on presenting your qualifications with precision and clarity. Stick to standard headings, clean formatting, and tailor your application for each role to maximize impact.

Remember: your resume isn't just a document—it's your first impression, your story, and your gateway to new opportunities. Optimizing it for ATSs while making it engaging for hiring managers is your key to standing out in a crowded job market.

Don't wait—apply these strategies today and take one step closer to landing your dream role!

Strategy Two. Explore Global Opportunities and Navigate the Connected Job Market with Confidence

Welcome to the era of global connectivity, where **remote work** has revolutionized professional landscapes! With platforms like LinkedIn connecting over a billion users worldwide, the job market has become a vibrant arena brimming with opportunities and competition. The exciting reality? You now have unparalleled access to positions that let you work from anywhere, breaking free from traditional geographic constraints and unlocking a world of possibilities.

Gone are the days when you had to search for a job limited to your city or state. Today, you're competing and collaborating with talented professionals from across the globe, each bringing diverse skills, perspectives, and experiences. This change creates a fairer system, offering many new opportunities you may not have considered. As remote work becomes the norm, companies are not bound by location when seeking top talent. Your dream job could be just a click away, no matter where you live.

The Benefits of a Global Job Search

Exploring global opportunities expands more than just your career options. It reshapes your worldview, sharpens your skillset, and broadens your professional network. Imagine working for an international company that introduces you to innovative practices, unique market dynamics, and creative problem-solving approaches you wouldn't encounter otherwise. This exposure enhances your cultural competency, adaptability, and understanding of global

> **This exposure enhances your cultural competency, adaptability, and understanding of global industries—all traits prized by employers.**

industries—all traits prized by employers.

Beyond professional growth, remote work empowers you to design a life that aligns with your aspirations. Whether you're drawn to the creative buzz of a bustling city or the serenity of a seaside village, you can create an environment that fuels productivity and inspiration. Stepping into the global market allows you to craft a career that reflects your ambitions and enables you to contribute to an interconnected world.

Practical Steps to Navigate the Global Job Market

To stand out in the competitive international job market, a strategic approach is essential. Here's how to shine:

- ▶ **Expand Your Digital Presence:** Optimize your LinkedIn profile by highlighting globally relevant skills like cross-cultural communication, project management, or technical expertise. Incorporate global keywords such as "international experience," "remote collaboration," or "virtual team management." Engage actively by joining LinkedIn groups, participating in discussions, and sharing insightful content. For example, join a group of remote marketing professionals. By sharing ideas and connecting with members, you could catch the attention of hiring managers seeking dynamic talent.
- ▶ **Leverage Remote Job Platforms:** Explore specialized platforms and use tools like We Work Remotely, Remote.co, and FlexJobs to find global opportunities. Set up tailored job alerts for roles that match your skills and interests. Tailor your resume and cover letter to reflect an understanding of the

company's global culture and values. For example, highlight specific international projects or collaborations you've been part of.

▸ **Highlight Multicultural Competencies:** Showcase global experiences by including study abroad programs, international team collaborations, or global project leadership. Demonstrate adaptability by emphasizing language skills, cultural awareness, and your ability to thrive in diverse environments. For example, you could write: "Led cross-functional teams across five time zones to launch a digital campaign that boosted brand awareness by 35 percent."

▸ **Network Across Borders:** Attend virtual events and participate in industry webinars, global conferences, and online meetups to connect with professionals worldwide. Send personalized messages expressing interest in potential collaborations. After an event, reach out to a speaker on LinkedIn and say something like, "I appreciated your insights on global marketing strategies. I'd love to stay connected and learn more about your work."

▸ **Prepare for Virtual Interviews:** Rehearse answering questions and familiarize yourself with video conferencing tools. Adapt your communication style by researching the company's cultural norms to align your approach with their values. For example, when interviewing with a Japanese company, demonstrate humility and teamwork, as these traits are highly valued.

Embrace the Journey

Diving into the global job market isn't just about landing a job—it's about embracing challenges, unlocking opportunities, and fueling your growth. Each application, interview, and networking interaction enriches your professional narrative and broadens your horizons.

Picture this: You secure a remote role with an international team, collaborating daily with colleagues from Germany, Brazil, and India. This dynamic environment pushes you to think creatively, adapt to diverse perspectives, and develop innovative solutions. The experience transforms your career and deepens your personal growth, setting the stage for a globally impactful journey.

Final Thoughts

This is your moment to step boldly into the global job market and let your unique talents shine. With the right strategies, you're not just another resume. You're a standout candidate brimming with potential, ambition, and a global mindset. The world is teeming with opportunities. Seize them, carve a career path that reflects your dreams, and celebrate every step of the journey.

Remember, the goal isn't just to secure a role. It's to thrive, grow, and take pride in being part of a vibrant tapestry of global talent. Your moment is here. Make it extraordinary!

Strategy Three. Capitalize on the Gig Economy by Showcasing Your Skills in a Flexible World

Welcome to the dynamic **gig economy**—a thriving landscape that has redefined modern work. From short-term projects to freelance opportunities on platforms like Upwork, Fiverr, and Uber, this ecosystem empowers you to craft a career that aligns with your lifestyle. The flexibility and independence are undeniable draws, offering the freedom to explore your passions and set your own path. Yet navigating this space requires strategy, especially if you're balancing gig work with long-term career aspirations.

The rise of freelancing has reshaped employment possibilities, opening doors to diverse industries and projects. While this expansion creates exciting opportunities, it also increases competition, with professionals worldwide vying for roles that offer autonomy and variety. For those seeking stability, gig work becomes a stepping stone—a powerful way to enrich your skills, expand your network, and position yourself for future success.

The gig economy doesn't diminish your value—it amplifies it.

Embracing the gig economy isn't about choosing flexibility over stability. It's about leveraging every project as a building block for growth.

Turning Gigs into Paths Forward

Embracing the gig economy isn't about choosing flexibility over stability. It's about leveraging every project as a building block for growth. Each assignment adds depth to your expertise, enhances your adaptability, and strengthens your professional narrative. These aren't just jobs. They're opportunities to showcase your creativity, resilience, and ability to excel in diverse environments.

Imagine this: A freelance graphic designer transitions into a full-time creative director role by presenting a **portfolio** of innovative branding projects. Or a freelance writer leverages a history of client success stories to land a content marketing manager position. These examples show how gig work can propel you toward your long-term goals.

Actionable Strategies for Thriving in the Gig Economy

To make the most of this vibrant landscape, here are key strategies to elevate your freelance experience and position yourself for lasting success:

- **Highlight Your Unique Skills:** Identify in-demand strengths. Whether it's web development, consulting, or social media strategy, know what sets you apart. Tailor your pitch by aligning your skills with the client's need for maximum impact. For example, instead of saying, "I'm a freelance writer," frame it as, "I'm a content strategist specializing in SEO-driven articles that boost engagement and drive results."

- **Build a Portfolio That Shines:** Showcase your work. Create a polished portfolio with visuals, metrics, and testimonials to highlight your impact. Choose the right platform and use tools like Behance or your website to professionally present your projects. Include before-and-after results or client feedback to show measurable success. For instance, a web developer could feature analytics showing how a redesigned site improved user engagement.

- **Network with Purpose:** Use LinkedIn, forums, and professional groups to connect with peers and potential clients. Establish thought leadership by sharing insights, commenting on posts, and actively participating in industry discussions. For example, join a LinkedIn group for digital marketers and contribute regularly. Sharing ideas and engaging in conversations positions you as a knowledgeable, approachable professional.

- **Leverage Flexible Scheduling:** Analyze how you spend your time and choose to dedicate specific hours to freelancing and others to skill-building or pursuing permanent roles. Balance your schedule effectively by implementing flexibility to align short-term work with long-term career goals. Plan your day around priorities, ensuring steady progress on multiple fronts. This disciplined approach keeps your freelance journey aligned with your broader aspirations.

- **Stay Ahead of Industry Trends:** Keep learning by monitoring changes in your field to stay competitive and identify emerging opportunities. Adapt proactively and leverage your knowledge to offer cutting-edge solutions. For example, if you're a digital marketer, staying informed about algorithm updates or trending platforms positions you as a forward-thinking candidate that clients trust.

Embrace the Journey

Freelancing doesn't just diversify your career—it strengthens your resilience, sharpens your skills, and enriches your story. Every project you tackle reflects your ability to innovate, adapt, and excel in diverse environments.

Picture this: A freelance app developer collaborates with global teams, gaining technical expertise as well as leadership and cross-cultural communication skills. When they apply for a full-time role, this unique experience sets them apart as a versatile, dynamic candidate.

Final Thoughts

The gig economy isn't just a trend. It's a powerful way to shape your future. By embracing its opportunities with intention and curiosity, you can create a fulfilling balance between flexibility and stability that aligns with your goals.

Your freelance journey isn't a collection of short-term gigs. It's a testament to your ambition, creativity, and adaptability. Every project adds to your skillset and showcases your potential. Take pride in the challenges you've overcome and the successes you've achieved. These experiences define your story and make you a standout candidate in any market.

Remember, this journey isn't just about the next gig or job. It's about celebrating your growth, fueling your ambition, and building a future filled with purpose and achievement. Your path is yours to carve. Make it extraordinary!

Strategy Four. Elevate Your Online Networking by Building Connections That Propel Your Career

Online networking has revolutionized how we connect, collaborate, and thrive in our careers. Platforms like LinkedIn are no longer just digital resumes—they've developed into dynamic hubs for building meaningful relationships, exchanging insights, and amplifying your professional story. With a few strategic clicks, you can join industry-specific groups, take part in insightful discussions, and connect with professionals across the globe. This digital evolution puts you in control of your career journey, showcasing your unique human potential.

Gone are the days of limiting networking to coffee chats or in-person events. Today's landscape offers virtual webinars, workshops, and panels hosted by companies and industry leaders that allow you to engage with experts and like-minded peers.

Gone are the days of limiting networking to coffee chats or in-person events. Today's landscape offers virtual webinars, workshops, and panels hosted by companies and industry leaders that allow you to engage with experts and like-minded peers. These events help you display your expertise and passion while making meaningful connections—all from the comfort of your own home. This shift eliminates logistical barriers, broadens your reach, and enhances your professional visibility.

Digital platforms also offer unparalleled access to insider knowledge and opportunities. By networking online, you can discover job leads, gain valuable industry insights, and secure **referrals** from professionals who recognize your potential. Referrals often serve as fast tracks to interviews, making authentic online engagement a vital career-advancement tool. Your participation enhances your visibility, builds credibility, and positions you as a standout in a competitive market.

Ask yourself: "What impression does my LinkedIn profile leave on someone viewing it for the first time?"

Ask yourself: "What impression does my LinkedIn profile leave on someone viewing it for the first time?"

Maximizing Your Online Networking Potential

Here are five actionable strategies to help you harness the full power of digital networking while showcasing your authenticity and ambition:

> ▶ **Polish Your Online Presence:** Craft an interesting profile and ensure your LinkedIn page is complete, professional, and engaging. Choose a confident-looking photo, write an authentic summary, and highlight your key skills and accomplishments. Show your story, which should reflect not just your expertise but also your passion and vision. For example: "Creative digital marketer specializing in data-driven campaigns that inspire engagement and drive growth. Passionate about turning analytics into actionable strategies that deliver real results."

> ▶ **Engage with Intention:** Be visible by actively participating and commenting on posts, sharing articles, and sparking

meaningful conversations that showcase your voice. Each thoughtful engagement ensures you remain relevant while reflecting your unique perspectives. For example, when a professional shares an update on industry trends, respond with "This aligns with recent patterns I've noticed in my work. I'd love to hear your perspective on how this trend might grow over the next year."

▶ **Join Industry-Specific Groups:** Find your community by engaging with groups that align with your career goals. Actively take part in discussions, ask insightful questions, and share your expertise. You can expand your reach by using these groups to stay informed and build relationships with industry insiders. You can do this by searching for LinkedIn groups relevant to your niche—whether in tech, education, or the creative arts—and contribute regularly to discussions, reinforcing your credibility and approachability.

▶ **Attend Virtual Events with Purpose:** Show up prepared by researching topics and speakers before attending webinars, panels, or workshops. Use these events to learn and make connections. Be sure to engage by asking thoughtful questions and connecting with attendees or speakers post-event to deepen your relationships. For example, after attending a panel on marketing innovation, message a speaker on LinkedIn and say, "I really appreciated your insights on audience segmentation during today's webinar. I'd love to stay connected and explore how your strategies could apply to my current projects."

▶ **Follow Up:** Keep the dialogue alive after you've made a connection by sending a personalized message that references your interaction. Express gratitude and outline potential avenues for collaboration. This strategy builds relationships because thoughtful follow-ups transform introductions into meaningful professional connections.

For example, you could write, "It was a pleasure meeting you during the digital marketing workshop. Our conversation about content strategy really resonated with me, and I look forward to staying connected."

Embrace the Power of Online Networking

Online networking is more than a way to expand your contact list—it's about creating a vibrant professional community that supports your growth and amplifies your success. Authentic engagement opens doors to collaboration, learning, and career-changing opportunities.

Picture this: You connect with a mentor who offers invaluable guidance or collaborate with a peer on an innovative project. These pivotal relationships often begin with simple actions—joining a group, attending an event, or contributing to a discussion. Each interaction is a step toward building a professional foundation that fuels your aspirations.

Take pride in your ability to navigate this digital landscape with purpose and confidence. Your voice matters, and your contributions can make a lasting impact. By embracing these strategies, you're not just advancing your career—you're shaping a journey rich with growth, collaboration, and success.

> **Your voice matters, and your contributions can make a lasting impact.**

Now is the time to act. Step into the digital networking space, cultivate meaningful connections, and build a future that aligns with your ambitions. The opportunities are endless—seize them boldly!

Strategy Five. Ace Video Interviews on Zoom and Leave a Lasting Impression

In today's fast-paced job market, companies rely on technology to streamline the hiring process. **Video interviews** and online assessments have become vital tools for evaluating candidates' skills, communication styles, and cultural fit. This shift provides you with a unique opportunity to showcase your best self from the comfort of your home—offering a chance to present your talents in a structured yet personal way that highlights your unique journey.

Platforms like Zoom, Microsoft Teams, and Google Meet have revolutionized the hiring landscape by offering flexible alternatives to in-person meetings. These tools allow you to connect with employers from anywhere, eliminating time and travel barriers while enabling you to focus on demonstrating your expertise.
By mastering the art of video interviews, you show that you're a forward-thinking, tech-savvy candidate who understands the value of human connections—an increasingly important trait for modern employers.

The rise of video interviews has expanded the talent pool for companies, offering opportunities to candidates regardless of location. For you, this is an exciting chance to access roles that align with your skills, no matter where you are. By embracing this global reach, you position yourself as a dynamic and adaptable candidate, highlighting your ability to thrive in today's interconnected, technology-driven workplace.

Mastering the Video Interview

To excel in video interviews and make a memorable impression, follow these five practical strategies:

1. **Set the Stage for Success:** Create a polished environment. Choose a quiet, well-lit space with a clean and neutral background to ensure the focus remains on you. A tidy workspace shows your attention to detail and professionalism. For example, instead of cluttered bookshelves or busy desks, opt for a simple background, like a neutral wall or an organized workspace. Adding a subtle touch, like a small plant, can showcase your personality without distraction.
2. **Test and Troubleshoot the Tech:** Prepare your tech in advance. Familiarize yourself with the platform you'll use for the interview. Do a trial run to check audio, video, and internet connection. Position the camera at eye level to maintain natural engagement. **Pro Tip:** have a backup device or hotspot ready in case of unexpected technical difficulties. This shows preparedness and problem-solving—important traits for employers to see.
3. **Practice Makes Perfect:** Rehearse your responses. Practice answering common interview questions confidently in front of the camera. Record yourself to identify areas for improvement, like pacing, tone, or body language. For example, for a question like "Tell me about a time you solved a challenging problem," keep your answer concise. Highlight your role and explain the positive outcome. Watching your practice video helps you refine your delivery and boosts confidence.
4. **Engage with Virtual Eye Contact:** Look at the camera while speaking to simulate eye contact with the interviewer. Avoid focusing on your image on the screen, as it can break the connection.

   Pro Tip: Place a sticky note near the camera with the reminder "Smile and engage." This keeps your expressions warm and inviting, ensuring the interviewer feels connected to you.

5. **Follow Up Thoughtfully:** Send a meaningful follow-up. Within twenty-four hours, send a personalized message thanking the interviewer for their time. Reference specific parts of the conversation to show genuine interest and reinforce your enthusiasm for the role. For example, you can write, "Thank you for discussing your team's innovative marketing strategies during our interview. I'm excited about the opportunity to contribute my skills to such a forward-thinking organization."

Embrace the Spotlight

Mastering video interviews isn't just about presenting your qualifications. It's about conveying your personality, enthusiasm, and adaptability in a virtual setting. With each successful interview, you prove your ability to thrive in today's hybrid work environments, reinforcing your value as a forward-thinking professional.

Take pride in the effort you invest in every step of the process. By embracing these tools and strategies, you'll navigate the hiring process with confidence and position yourself as a standout candidate ready to make a meaningful impact.

Step into the spotlight, embrace the opportunity to connect, and let your unique talents shine. The professional world is waiting for you—seize the moment and leave your mark!

ESSENTIAL TAKEAWAYS
FOR THRIVING IN THE AGE OF AI

In the age of AI, your creativity is your superpower. It sets you apart as a dynamic, indispensable candidate.

Showcase Your Human Creativity

AI is good at analyzing information, but it can't replace human creativity and insight. Highlight your creative problem-solving in applications, interviews, or networking conversations to show your irreplaceable contribution. Your unique ability to innovate is what makes you stand out in a technology-driven world.

Fuel your success by showing employers that your creativity is not only a skill but a driving force behind progress and problem-solving in any organization.

Cultivate Genuine Connections

In today's digital-first world, building authentic relationships is more crucial than ever. While AI can analyze vast amounts of data, it lacks the **emotional intelligence** to foster real human connections. It's your empathy, sincerity, and communication skills that will leave a lasting impression. Whether it's through a thoughtful LinkedIn message or a personalized follow-up email after an interview, meaningful engagement helps you build trust and elevate your professional presence.

Invest in relationships that resonate with others. Your ability to connect on a human level is what makes you unforgettable.

Adapt to Digital Landscapes with Confidence

In the ever-evolving landscape of AI-driven hiring, your adaptability is your greatest asset. The new tools, such as ATSs and video interviews, are opportunities to show resilience and forward-thinking leadership. By mastering these platforms, you position yourself as a candidate who is not only keeping pace but also leading the way into the future.

Embrace technological change with confidence and clarity—this demonstrates your ability to thrive in the digital world, giving you the competitive edge in any job market.

Leverage the Power of Emotional Intelligence

AI may excel in data, but it cannot navigate the complex human emotions and interpersonal dynamics that fuel effective leadership and collaboration. Your emotional intelligence—your empathy, active listening, and conflict resolution skills—sets you apart as a well-rounded, capable team member. Share examples from your experiences where you've successfully collaborated or led through challenging situations to demonstrate this critical strength.

Show how your emotional intelligence elevates the teams and environments you're a part of. It's the foundation for sustainable success in any workplace.

Craft and Communicate Your Unique Value

In a world dominated by data, your individuality makes you irreplaceable. Reflect on your unique qualities—your passions, experiences, and personal drive—and use them to craft a compelling narrative that reflects your **personal brand**. Whether through a tailored resume, an engaging LinkedIn profile, or a confident interview, communicate your authentic value in a way that makes employers see you as an integral part of their success.

> **Your individuality is your strength. In a sea of resumes and applications, your personal story makes you memorable, sets you apart, and ensures you make the impact you deserve.**

Your individuality is your strength. In a sea of resumes and applications, your personal story makes you memorable, sets you apart, and ensures you make the impact you deserve.

By harnessing your human qualities—creativity, connection, adaptability, emotional intelligence, and individuality—you can stand out in the age of AI. Now is the time to embrace these principles, craft your personal narrative, and step boldly into a future where technology complements your unique talents.

YOUR NEXT STEPS: EXCELLING IN A DIGITAL WORLD

Congratulations on completing this chapter! Now it's time to turn these insights into action. These steps will help you refine your human edge, amplify your professional presence, and navigate the evolving AI-driven job market with confidence. Let's take the first steps toward standing out and thriving in this digital age.

1. Highlight Your Human Edge

Showcase your creativity, empathy, and adaptability in tangible ways that leave a lasting impact.

▸ Reflect on a specific instance where your creativity or emotional intelligence made a meaningful difference in your professional or personal life.
▸ Craft your story around the positive changes or measurable outcomes your actions inspired and be ready to share it in interviews, cover letters, or networking conversations.

Pro Tip: Focus on impact—frame your story to highlight how your unique strengths fueled results and brought about positive change.

2. Optimize for Digital Hiring Tools

Maximize your visibility by embracing AI-driven systems to highlight your strengths.

- ▶ Dedicate thirty minutes to review and refine your resume for ATSs. Ensure it's optimized with keywords from job descriptions and maintains clean, minimalist formatting.
- ▶ Practice for a video interview on platforms like Zoom or Microsoft Teams. Focus on your body language, tone, and background to make a lasting professional impression.

Pro Tip: Use tools like Jobscan to test your resume's compatibility with ATSs and fine-tune it for each role.

3. Cultivate Genuine Connections

Engage with others authentically to expand your network and foster meaningful relationships.

- ▶ Reach out to three professionals in your field on LinkedIn this week. Craft personalized messages that express genuine interest in their work and ask thoughtful questions to spark meaningful conversations.
- ▶ Follow up after networking events—whether virtual or in-person—by referencing specific parts of your conversation to keep the connection alive.

Pro Tip: Share or comment on relevant industry content to remain visible and engaged with your network.

4. Embrace Continuous Learning

Stay ahead of the curve by expanding your skillset and embracing new opportunities for growth.

- ▶ Identify a digital tool, skill, or AI-related topic that's relevant to your industry and commit to learning more about it.
- ▶ Set a timeline to complete an online course, attend a workshop, or read a book that aligns with your professional goals.

Pro Tip: Apply your new knowledge to real-world projects or conversations to reinforce your learning and demonstrate your adaptability.

5. Craft Your Unique Narrative

Build a compelling personal brand that clearly communicates your value.

- ▶ Write or update your LinkedIn summary to reflect your unique strengths, career aspirations, and the skills that set you apart.
- ▶ Draft a professional pitch that emphasizes your individuality and practice delivering it confidently in interviews or networking events.

Pro Tip: Tell a story—use a brief anecdote that showcases your creativity, problem-solving, or resilience to make your pitch unforgettable.

YOUR JOURNEY STARTS HERE

These actions aren't just tasks—they're stepping stones to becoming an irreplaceable professional in a tech-driven job market. By blending your human qualities with a strategic embrace of technology, you position yourself as a candidate who's not just relevant but also irreplaceable.

Take the first step today. Your unique edge is your superpower. Use it to make a lasting impression and build the career you've always envisioned!

Trust your instincts, embrace your values, and pursue opportunities that align with your unique potential.

CHAPTER 2

DEFINING YOUR NONNEGOTIABLES

Building a Career That Honors Your Values

Your **nonnegotiables** are more than just preferences. They're the foundation of who you are. They represent the **core values** and priorities that guide your decisions, shaping a career that aligns with your goals, ideals, and vision for the future. Embracing these nonnegotiables isn't merely about identifying what you want; it's about recognizing what you deserve.

Pause for a moment and reflect on the times you've felt fulfilled. Perhaps your creativity surged, your contributions gained genuine recognition, or your work aligned with your deepest values. These moments aren't random—they are powerful clues to the environments, relationships, and opportunities that bring out your best self.

In today's fast-paced job market, the pressure to compromise or conform to external expectations can be overwhelming. The fear of missing out, the urge to accept the first offer, or the allure of a high-paying role can cloud your judgment. But when you take the time to define your nonnegotiables, you gain clarity and confidence. You see the job market not as a race or a gamble but as a purposeful journey where each step is in line with your values.

> **You see the job market not as a race or a gamble but as a purposeful journey where each step is in line with your values.**

OWNING YOUR WORTH

When you identify and stand firm in your nonnegotiables, you send a powerful message—not just to potential employers but also to yourself. You declare that your values, your strengths, and your vision are worth honoring. This isn't about arrogance or rigidity; it's about self-respect. By setting clear boundaries, you invite opportunities that align with your goals and create space for both personal and professional growth.

> **When you identify and stand firm in your nonnegotiables, you send a powerful message—not just to potential employers but also to yourself.**

Imagine stepping into an interview prepared to answer questions and fully aware of what you're seeking. You're not only selling your skills—you're assessing whether this role fits your vision for a fulfilling career. This mindset transforms you into a stronger candidate and sets the stage for a mutually rewarding relationship between you and your employer.

THE COST OF COMPROMISE

Compromising on your nonnegotiables might seem like an easy way to succeed, but it often leads to dissatisfaction and burnout. Think back to a time when you accepted a role or project that didn't align with your core values. Maybe you felt disconnected, unappreciated, or unfulfilled. These moments teach us a crucial lesson: the alignment between your career and your principles isn't optional—it's essential for sustained motivation and joy.

By honoring your nonnegotiables, you ensure that every step of your journey reflects your true self. While no role is perfect, choosing environments that value your contributions and nurture your potential makes all the difference.

ENTERING THE JOB MARKET WITH PURPOSE

Approaching your career with purpose transforms the job search from a daunting process into an empowering journey. Each resume you send, each conversation you engage in, and each interview you attend becomes an opportunity to showcase your skills and your authenticity. Employers don't hire for qualifications—they seek individuals who bring creativity, empathy, and resilience to their teams.

By focusing on your nonnegotiables, you build a career that celebrates your individuality.

By focusing on your nonnegotiables, you build a career that celebrates your individuality. You're not just filling a position; you're carving out a space where your unique perspective and talents can thrive. This intentionality fosters a sense of pride and satisfaction that extends far beyond the workplace, enriching your sense of purpose and connection in every area of life.

A MOMENT OF REFLECTION

Before we dive deeper into the strategies that will guide your journey, take a moment to reflect on what matters most to you. Let these questions anchor your thoughts as you explore your nonnegotiables and shape your path forward:

- ▶ **Discovering Core Values:** Think back to a time when you felt truly fulfilled—at work or in life. What specific elements of that experience align with your core values, and how can you seek similar opportunities in your career?
- ▶ **Setting Your Nonnegotiables:** What are your top three nonnegotiables in a career? How do these priorities shape the way you approach your job search and evaluate opportunities?
- ▶ **Overcoming Compromise:** Reflect on a situation where you compromised on a career decision. How did it affect your fulfillment, and what lessons can you use to align your future choices with your values?

As you reflect on these questions, remember: every step you take toward understanding and honoring your nonnegotiables is a step toward a career that genuinely aligns with who you are. Embrace this journey with pride and confidence. Your values are your compass, guiding you toward opportunities where you can thrive and make a real impact.

FIVE STRATEGIES TO
SHAPE YOUR FUTURE CAREER PATH

Ready to take control of your career? Here are five powerful strategies to plan your future and unlock your full potential.

Strategy One. Recognizing Your Value: Defining What Matters in Your Career

Defining your core values can feel like piecing together a puzzle. Are your goals inspiring enough to drive you forward? Do they align with what truly excites you, or are they shaped by external expectations? Beneath these questions lies a deeper truth: the values guiding your professional life should also resonate deeply in your personal relationships. While this process may seem overwhelming, understanding what matters most is vital to building a career that is true to your authentic self.

Reflect on the moments in your life when you felt genuinely fulfilled. Think back to those times when you felt most alive. What were you doing? Who were you with? And why did those moments hold such meaning? Your memories are more than mere nostalgia. They reveal the principles that shape your true aspirations.

In my book *Retail Pride*, I shared the "Top 10 Reasons We Love Working in Retail," and the number one reason was the joy we create. This principle resonates deeply with me: when we focus on bringing joy to others—whether through our work or personal interactions—we connect with something far beyond ourselves. It's not just about completing tasks; it's about making an impact that fosters pride and purpose.

For example, imagine a retail associate helping a customer find the perfect gift. Their work creates more than just a transaction—it builds a moment of connection and happiness. For someone like me, who deeply values spreading positivity, this simple interaction embodies a core value. When our actions align with these values, our work becomes a source of fulfillment and motivation.

To uncover your own values, try keeping a "joy journal." Write down moments when you felt energized, inspired, or accomplished. Over time, you'll see patterns—perhaps you thrive in problem-solving, find fulfillment in helping others, or excel in teamwork. These patterns illuminate the values that define your decisions and reveal what truly matters to you.

This process is not about perfection; it's about discovery. Approach it without judgment and allow your experiences to shape your understanding of who you are. As you evolve, your values may deepen, strengthening your sense of purpose and potential.

When your career aligns with your values, your confidence and capabilities grow together. This creates a positive feedback loop—where confidence fuels skill and success breeds pride. Over time, this momentum will empower you to embrace challenges and achieve goals that once seemed out of reach.

> **When your career aligns with your values, your confidence and capabilities grow together.**

Making Values-Based Career Choices

To ensure your next role aligns with your values, ask meaningful questions during interviews. These questions will not only help you assess the role's fit but also show your thoughtful approach:

- ▶ What does success look like in this role, and how is it measured over time?
- ▶ Can you describe the team dynamics and company culture?
- ▶ How does this role contribute to the company's mission, and what meaningful impacts have team members made in the past?

- What opportunities for growth and development exist, and how are they supported?
- What challenges does the team face, and how do they collaborate to overcome them?
- How is feedback provided, and how does it foster an ongoing dialogue?
- What strategies does the company use to encourage collaboration, and how are they evaluated?

Final Thoughts...
a Career Rooted in Your Values

By asking these questions, you ensure that the role you pursue truly aligns with your values and aspirations. This approach is about more than landing a job—it's about building a career that resonates with who you are, both personally and professionally.

As you reflect on your journey, celebrate the values that define you and the pride that comes from honoring them. Staying true to yourself helps you achieve success, and it fosters a work culture that celebrates authenticity, connection, and growth.

Your path to fulfillment begins with clarity, confidence, and the courage to prioritize what truly matters. Trust your instincts, embrace your values, and pursue opportunities that align with your unique potential. This is your moment—make it count!

Trust your instincts, embrace your values, and pursue opportunities that align with your unique potential.

Strategy Two. Embracing Progress: Charting Your Path to Professional Fulfillment

Harness your unique qualities and human pride to elevate your career. When you approach challenges with confidence and enthusiasm, you're more likely to embrace responsibilities that foster growth. Pride in your abilities enables you to highlight your achievements and strengths, which enhances your reputation and unlocks promotions and opportunities. By consistently demonstrating excellence, reliability, and integrity, you lay a firm foundation for lasting success.

Strategic **career mapping** is crucial to realizing your aspirations. Define your goals clearly and break them down into actionable steps. For example, if becoming a senior leader is your goal, identify the skills, training, and experiences you need. Take on challenging projects, seek mentorship, and invest in **continuous learning** to prepare yourself for future roles.

Flexibility is equally important. Careers evolve, and unforeseen opportunities often arise. If a new interest complements your broader goals, embrace it—even if it wasn't part of your initial plan. Being open to new experiences ensures you stay adaptable and aligned with your objectives.

Each deliberate step brings you closer to a career that reflects your aspirations and promotes your personal growth.

Regular self-assessment is key to staying on course. Reflect on whether your decisions support your long-term aspirations. If a project or opportunity doesn't align with your strategy, weigh its potential impact carefully. This intentional approach ensures your efforts remain focused and meaningful.

Aligning your career path with your values creates a journey that is both impactful and fulfilling. Each deliberate step brings you closer to a career that reflects your aspirations and promotes your personal growth.

Essential Topics to Discuss During Interviews

To ensure alignment with your goals, consider these essential topics during interviews:

- ▶ **Career Growth:** Ask, "What paths exist for this role, and how do team members advance?" This uncovers opportunities for progression and highlights the company's commitment to growth.
- ▶ **Compensation:** Inquire, "How is compensation structured, and how often are salary reviews conducted?" This clarifies fairness and recognition practices.
- ▶ **Benefits:** Ask, "What benefits support employee well-being and balance?" This reveals the company's dedication to its workforce.
- ▶ **Skill Development:** Explore, "What training programs does the company offer to enhance skills?" Development opportunities are crucial for growth.
- ▶ **Promotion Opportunities:** Ask, "How does the company evaluate candidates for promotion?" This offers insight into **fairness** and **transparency** in advancement.
- ▶ **Feedback and Performance:** Discuss, "How is feedback provided, and how is performance evaluated?" A strong feedback culture fosters improvement.
- ▶ **Networking and Growth:** Ask, "Are there opportunities to attend industry events or conferences?" This reflects the company's investment in broader career development.

▶ **Vision for the Role:** Inquire, "How do you see this role evolving over the next few years?" This helps align your goals with the company's future direction.

These thoughtful questions reflect your proactive approach and commitment to finding a role that aligns with your aspirations. They also provide valuable insight into how well the company's culture supports your values and professional growth.

Final Thoughts

Embracing pride in your abilities and strategically planning your career sets you on the path to fulfillment. By asking insightful questions and pursuing aligned opportunities, you take control of your professional journey. Stay adaptable, reflective, and intentional, and you'll build a career that reflects your values and potential.

Take pride in your journey, trust your instincts, and create a future that honors your worth and ambitions.

Remember, your career is more than just a collection of roles—it's a reflection of your unique strengths and aspirations. Take pride in your journey, trust your instincts, and create a future that honors your worth and ambitions.

Strategy Three. Redefining Balance: Unlocking Your Human Potential

The phrase "work-life balance" is often overused but seldom understood. Rather than viewing **balance** as a rigid separation between work and personal life, think of it as a fluid integration where career, relationships, health, and passions coexist in harmony. This approach creates a life that honors your well-being and potential while fostering purpose and satisfaction.

True balance reflects human pride by prioritizing what truly matters. By setting clear boundaries, you allow your career to complement—

True balance reflects human pride by prioritizing what truly matters.

not overwhelm—your personal life. This alignment nurtures activities that energize you, cultivating well-being and a sense of accomplishment that extends beyond professional success. Balance, in this context, becomes a tool to create a life filled with joy, intention, and fulfillment.

Achieving balance often requires the courage to say no. Declining additional responsibilities isn't about avoiding opportunities; it's about protecting your time and energy for what matters. This conscious discernment prevents burnout, enabling you to focus on the relationships, health, and passions that bring you fulfillment. It's an act of alignment with your values, setting the stage for both personal and professional growth.

Championing balance is more than just a concept—it's a guiding principle. By committing to this, you embrace a resilient, purpose-driven life aligned with your aspirations. Advocating for flexible schedules or remote work fosters an environment that supports your lifestyle, enhances collaboration, and nurtures mutual respect. These efforts ensure your needs are met while also contributing to greater productivity and teamwork.

As you navigate your career, make balance a cornerstone of your success. Doing so will shape a fulfilling journey marked by achievements that honor both your personal and professional ideals.

Key Questions to Assess a Company's Commitment to Balance

- ▶ **How does the company support balance at all levels?** Investigate how company policies and practices integrate employee well-being into the culture.

- ▶ **What is the company's stance on remote work and flexibility?** Assess how the company adapts to modern work-life integration needs and how it aligns with your priorities.

- ▶ **How do you prevent burnout?** Learn whether the organization actively promotes mental health and sustainable productivity.

- ▶ **How are achievements recognized and celebrated?** Gauge whether the company values employee contributions and fosters morale.

- ▶ **What resources exist for personal development?** Explore the support provided to balance personal and professional aspirations.

- ▶ **Can you provide examples of flexibility in action?** Look for tangible proof of the company's commitment to accommodating employee needs.

- ▶ **What are the workload and expectations for after-hours responses?** Explain the role's demands and how the company maintains boundaries to ensure sustainability.

- ▶ **To what extent do you grant autonomy in managing responsibilities?** Determine the level of independence and trust offered within the role.

- ▶ **How does the company address balance concerns?** Does the company encourage open dialogue to resolve work-life challenges?

Final Thoughts

Balance isn't a fixed destination; it's a dynamic journey requiring ongoing reflection and action. By asking these thoughtful questions, you uncover the layers of a company's culture and its commitment to harmony. This inquiry not only helps you align with your personal values but also contributes to fostering a balanced environment for everyone.

Engage with confidence, let your human pride guide you, and prioritize roles that honor your values and aspirations. Aligning your career with your needs is an act of courage and clarity, paving the way for a fulfilling path that supports your potential and well-being.

> **Engage with confidence, let your human pride guide you, and prioritize roles that honor your values and aspirations.**

Strategy Four. Selecting Your Champion: The Power of Thoughtful Supervision

The saying "People don't leave companies; they leave bosses" holds true, and research backs it up. But let's shift this perspective. Instead of focusing on poor supervisors, let's empower ourselves with the belief that **we can choose our boss**. Thoughtfully selecting a supervisor can revolutionize your work experience and elevate your career to new heights.

This is your journey, and understanding what to look for in a leader can make all the difference. Evaluating leadership styles, values, and support systems helps you identify a supervisor who aligns with your goals and nurtures your growth.

Why does this matter so deeply? Your relationship with your supervisor is a key determinant of your job satisfaction and career trajectory. A strong supervisor doesn't just set the tone for your work environment; they act as a mentor, an advocate, and a guide who shapes your development and success.

Imagine waking up each day eager to work alongside a supervisor who celebrates your achievements, supports you through challenges, and empowers you to evolve. A positive relationship fuels motivation, productivity, and job satisfaction. A toxic leader can lead to burnout, frustration, and stagnation. Choosing the right leader is essential for long-term success and fulfillment.

> **Your supervisor can be your greatest ally or a significant barrier, so making a thoughtful decision is critical.**

Your supervisor can be your greatest ally or a significant barrier, so making a thoughtful decision is critical. This isn't just about getting a job—it's about building a career that aligns with your aspirations, guided by leaders who inspire, support, and uplift you.

During interviews, observe potential supervisors. Ask questions that reveal their leadership style, how they give feedback, and how they handle conflict. Look for concrete examples that show how they've supported their team's growth and navigated adversity. This conversation should be central to your decision-making process.

Prioritizing a supportive and empowering supervisor isn't just part of the job search—it's an investment in a career that nurtures your potential and leads to fulfillment.

Key Questions to Understand
a Supervisor's Leadership Style

- **How has your leadership style evolved, and what experiences shaped it?** This provides insight into their adaptability and commitment to growth.
- **How do you deliver feedback to promote growth? Can you share an example of its impact?** Understanding their approach to feedback showcases their focus on development.
- **What skills do you prioritize in your team, and how do you help members develop them?** This reveals how they cultivate strengths and nurture talent.
- **Can you describe a recent team conflict and how you managed it? What did you learn?** Their response highlights how they handle challenges and foster team morale.
- **What professional development opportunities do you offer, and what results have you seen?** This shows their commitment to advancing team members' careers.
- **How do you mentor team members with long-term aspirations? Can you provide an example?** Mentorship shows their investment in individual growth.
- **What leadership challenges have shaped you, and how did they enhance your team's resilience?** This delves into their problem-solving abilities and leadership development.

Making the Right Choice

These questions aren't just a checklist. They are your pathway to understanding whether a potential supervisor aligns with your values and needs. By having these candid conversations, you take control of your career path and ensure it's guided by someone who truly supports and inspires you.

Remember, your supervisor plays a pivotal role in your professional life. Choosing the right one is more than securing a job. It's about crafting a fulfilling career that aligns with your values, unlocks your potential, and sets you on a path to success. Thoughtful leadership selection ensures a brighter, more empowering future. Choose wisely and build a relationship that propels you toward your goals!

Strategy Five. Beyond the Application: Assessing Employers for Career Growth

The job market has undergone a dramatic transformation, driven by economic shifts, cultural changes, and technological advancements. Getting a job in this tough market means more than just applying; you need to make a plan, build self-confidence, and know your strengths. Instead of waiting for opportunities, take control by actively seeking employers who resonate with your values and **aspirations**.

In today's market, shaped by AI, shifting consumer behavior, and global trends, it's crucial to assess the financial stability of potential employers. A company's financial health affects job security, career growth, and the work environment itself. Researching a company's performance, resilience, and approach to challenges will help you identify organizations that are prepared to thrive in the face of adversity.

Researching a company's performance, resilience, and approach to challenges will help you identify organizations that are prepared to thrive in the face of adversity.

Planning ahead gives you control and confidence to make smart career choices. It shows employers your commitment to **stability** and **growth**, signaling that you're ready to contribute substantially and strategically.

During interviews, demonstrate your insight by asking thoughtful questions about the company's financial health, growth plans, and resilience. For example, asking about their strategies in response to economic shifts or investments in employee development signals your focus on finding a supportive and forward-thinking employer.

This mindset reflects a deep sense of self-worth and resilience, guiding you toward roles that align with your values. By seeking clarity and purpose in your job search, you shape a career that benefits both you and your future employer.

Key Questions to Evaluate Employers

▶ **How does the company maintain financial stability and generate revenue?** Understanding how a company generates income and handles economic changes gives you insight into its long-term viability.

▶ **How has the company handled workforce reductions during past challenges?** Assess how the company treats its employees in tough times. Look for examples of support, retraining, or outplacement programs.

▶ **What is the company's growth strategy for the next five years?** A clear vision for the future shows stability and potential for career advancement. Learn how teams contribute to the company's goals.

▶ **How does leadership communicate financial health to employees?** Transparency builds trust. Ask about communication channels, such as town halls, newsletters, and how leadership encourages employee feedback.

▶ **What is the typical tenure of employees, and why do they stay?** High retention rates suggest strong leadership and job satisfaction. Inquire about internal mobility, culture, and the company's growth opportunities.

- ▶ **What sets this company apart from competitors in performance and employee experience?** Identify what makes the company unique—innovation, inclusive policies, or strong loyalty programs—that contribute to employee retention and satisfaction.
- ▶ **What initiatives drive innovation and maintain industry competitiveness?** Innovation is key to long-term success. Ask about R&D investments and how employees are involved in shaping key decisions.

BONUS Questions for Senior Leadership

- ▶ **What is the board's approach to inclusion and diversity?** A diverse board shows the company values a variety of perspectives. Inquire about representation across demographics and their strategies for inclusivity.
- ▶ **How do employees influence board decisions?** Companies that encourage employee input are more likely to foster a collaborative, open environment. Ask about mechanisms like surveys or focus groups.
- ▶ **How does the board assess its effectiveness?** Accountability signals strong leadership. Ask how the board evaluates its performance and ensures continuous improvement.
- ▶ **What initiatives promote diversity beyond the board?** A diverse leadership pipeline ensures inclusivity across the organization. Learn about mentorship programs or strategies for elevating underrepresented groups.

Taking Charge of Your Career

Asking these questions shows your proactive approach to aligning with employers who reflect your goals, values, and aspirations. This effort isn't just about landing a job; it's about choosing a workplace that champions your growth and empowers your potential.

Your job search is a journey toward alignment, fulfillment, and success. Approach the process with confidence and self-respect, and let your pride

Your job search is a journey toward alignment, fulfillment, and success.

guide you to a workplace where you can thrive. The future is yours to shape; it's filled with opportunities to excel, grow, and contribute.

ESSENTIAL TAKEAWAYS FOR DEFINING YOUR PATH

Discovering your core values is the foundation of aligning your career with your authentic self. Reflecting on moments when you felt joy, fulfillment, or deep satisfaction reveals the guiding principles that shape your aspirations. With this clarity, you can make career choices that resonate deeply with your sense of identity. Honoring these values allows you to position yourself in roles that amplify your potential, ensuring your career journey is meaningful, rewarding, and aligned with your deepest priorities.

Strategically Map Your Career Journey

A career built on intention and adaptability forms a powerful, purpose-driven path. Break long-term aspirations into manageable milestones and regularly assess your progress to ensure alignment with evolving goals. Flexibility allows you to embrace unexpected opportunities, enriching your journey with new experiences. This thoughtful approach not only keeps you motivated but also empowers you to overcome challenges, pursue your ambitions with purpose, and remain resilient in the face of obstacles.

Balance Personal Fulfillment with Professional Success

True balance integrates personal fulfillment with professional success, creating a harmonious and sustainable life. You foster well-being and satisfaction by setting clear boundaries and prioritizing activities that energize and inspire you. This balance enriches both your career and your overall sense of purpose, empowering long-term happiness and resilience. Prioritizing balance ensures that your professional achievements complement, rather than overshadow, your personal values and aspirations.

Select Supervisors Who Inspire and Empower You

The right supervisor plays a pivotal role in shaping your career satisfaction and growth. Evaluating their leadership style, values, and support systems during interviews ensures alignment with your goals. A supportive supervisor fosters resilience, collaboration, and growth, creating an environment where you can excel. By prioritizing leaders who inspire and empower you, you form a partnership that nurtures both professional success and personal fulfillment.

Evaluate Employers with Purpose and Precision

Researching potential employers helps you make informed decisions that align with your values and aspirations. Investigating a company's culture, stability, and growth strategies provides insight into whether it offers the right environment and opportunities. Asking thoughtful questions during interviews shows your proactive approach and ensures the organization aligns with your career goals. This intentional process positions you for success in a workplace that reflects your worth and supports your potential.

YOUR NEXT STEPS: ALIGNING WITH YOUR VALUES

Now that you've gained insights into the power of clarity and confidence in shaping your career, it's time to take meaningful action. Use these strategies to align your professional journey with your core values, aspirations, and long-term goals. By focusing on self-discovery and purposeful planning, you will create a career path that reflects your unique potential and priorities. Here's a step-by-step overview of what we've discussed in this chapter so you can start designing your ideal career path.

1. Define Your Core Values

Discover what drives your fulfillment and shapes your career decisions.

- ▶ Reflect on a time in your career or personal life when you felt deeply fulfilled.
- ▶ Identify three values that played a role during that experience and write them down.

Action Step: Journal how these values can guide your future career choices. Consider how you can integrate them into your daily work and long-term goals.

2. Create a Strategic Career Map

Design a roadmap that connects your aspirations with actionable steps.

- ▶ Outline your long-term career goal, whether it's advancing to a leadership position, transitioning into a new industry, or mastering a specific skill.

- Break this goal into three to five smaller milestones, each with its own timeline.

Action Step: Write down one immediate action you can take this week to move closer to your first milestone.

3. Identify and Honor Your Nonnegotiables

Clarify the priorities that matter most to you in your career and life.

- List your top three nonnegotiables for a job, such as work-life balance, opportunities for growth, or alignment with personal values.
- Reflect on how these priorities will guide the roles and companies you pursue.

Action Step: Use your list to evaluate a current or future job opportunity. Does it meet your standards?

4. Evaluate Supervisors and Work Environments

Ensure alignment with leadership and culture that supports your growth.

- Think about a time when a supervisor positively (or negatively) influenced your career. What traits made the difference?
- During your next job interview, prepare two thoughtful questions to assess their leadership style and company culture.

Action Step: Draft and practice asking a key question, such as "How do you support your team members' professional development and personal well-being?"

5. Align Your Job Search with Your Values

Take a strategic and intentional approach to your career opportunities.

- ▶ Research a potential employer's mission, values, and culture by exploring their website, employee reviews, and public statements.
- ▶ Tailor your resume and cover letter to highlight how your values and skills align with the organization's goals.

Action Step: Apply to one job this week where the company's values resonate with your own. Include a specific example in your application that reflects this alignment.

YOUR PATH, YOUR CHOICE

Defining your career path begins with self-awareness, thoughtful planning, and an unwavering commitment to your values. These actions empower you to approach the job market with clarity and confidence, ensuring each step you take leads to meaningful and impactful opportunities.

> **Defining your career path begins with self-awareness, thoughtful planning, and an unwavering commitment to your values.**

Trust in your ability to create a fulfilling career aligned with your authentic self. With these tools, you're not just pursuing jobs—you're building a future rooted in purpose, pride, and personal satisfaction.

Let your journey begin!

While your qualifications may get you in the door, your ability to connect, empathize, and engage with a team's values and culture is what sets you apart.

CHAPTER 3

AMPLIFYING THE POWER OF STORYTELLING

Elevating Your Career Narrative for Success

Storytelling is one of humanity's greatest gifts. It allows us to preserve experiences, share insights, and pass wisdom across generations. At its core, storytelling connects us, builds empathy, and creates a shared understanding that transcends differences. When applied to your professional life, storytelling becomes a bridge between who you are and the opportunities that align with your vision.

In today's digital-first job market, the power of your personal narrative has never been more crucial. Resumes and applications often reduce you to bullet points—highlighting accomplishments without context and overlooking the challenges, resilience, and growth that shaped those achievements. Storytelling lets you reclaim this missing depth. It enables you to present yourself not as a collection of qualifications but as a dynamic, multidimensional individual, bringing creativity, authenticity, and purpose to every interaction.

Your story is your greatest asset. It reveals not only what you've done but who you are, why you care, and how you approach the world. It highlights the connections between your values and your work, the lessons you've learned, and the vision you bring to every endeavor. Sharing your story builds trust, sparks collaboration, and opens doors in ways no algorithm ever could.

> **Your story is your greatest asset. It reveals not only what you've done but who you are, why you care, and how you approach the world.**

Think back to a time when someone's story captivated you—whether it was a colleague sharing their career journey, a friend overcoming a challenge, or a speaker who inspired you to dream bigger. What made that story resonate? It wasn't just the facts; it was the emotion, the relatability, and the courage to share a piece of their humanity. This is the power you hold when you share your own story.

THE COMPETITIVE EDGE IN A DIGITAL JOB MARKET

In a world where algorithms sift through applications and automated responses dominate hiring processes, storytelling sets you apart. It lets you bypass the impersonal and establish real connections. Whether in a networking conversation, an interview, or a cover letter, your ability to weave your experiences into a compelling

> **In a world where algorithms sift through applications and automated responses dominate hiring processes, storytelling sets you apart.**

narrative makes a lasting impression. Employers aren t just looking for skills—they're searching for people who embody adaptability, creativity, and the drive to make a difference.

When you craft your story with care, you highlight these qualities in ways that resonate deeply. You demonstrate your ability to reflect on your experiences, adapt to challenges, and find purpose in your work. More importantly, storytelling empowers you to show how your values align with the mission of the organization, which creates a sense of shared purpose that transcends transactional hiring practices.

TURNING YOUR JOURNEY INTO YOUR STRENGTH

Your journey—complete with its challenges, triumphs. and lessons—uniquely positions you for success. The obstacles you've overcome reveal your resilience; the risks you've taken showcase your courage; the opportunities you've embraced highlight your adaptability. Each element of your story adds dimension to your professional narrative, transforming it into a powerful force for connection and inspiration.

When you approach your career as a storyteller, you take control of how you're perceived.

This isn't about embellishment; it's about reframing your experiences with pride and clarity. It's about recognizing the inherent value in your story and using it to communicate your potential. When you approach your career as a storyteller, you take control of how you're perceived. You craft the narrative, ensuring it reflects not only your achievements but your character, vision, and unique contributions.

REFLECT AND BEGIN YOUR JOURNEY

Before diving into strategies to craft your professional narrative, take a moment to reflect on your story. These reflections will anchor you as you begin to articulate and refine your career journey:

- ▶ **Uncovering Your Strengths:** Think of a time when you faced a significant challenge. How did you overcome it, and what strengths did you discover in yourself? How can this story reflect your value to a potential employer?
- ▶ **Defining Your Mission:** What motivates you in your career? Is there a moment or experience that shaped your professional purpose? How does this mission align with the roles or companies you're pursuing?
- ▶ **Connecting Through Authenticity:** Reflect on a time when sharing your story created a meaningful connection. What made that moment impactful, and how can you bring that same authenticity to your professional narrative?

As you explore these questions, remember: your story isn't just a recounting of events—it's an expression of your humanity, your purpose, and your potential. Let's unlock the transformative power of storytelling together to elevate your career, connect with others, and inspire the future you envision. Your journey starts here, with your story leading the way.

MASTER THE ART OF STORYTELLING: FIVE STRATEGIES TO IMPRESS AND INSPIRE

Learning how to tell your story can be intimidating, but it doesn't have to be! Here are five strategies to help you leverage the power of storytelling to connect with prospective companies.

Strategy One. Cultivating Authentic Connections: Harnessing the Power of Emotional Intelligence

In today's highly competitive job market, **emotional intelligence** is the key to standing out. While your qualifications may get you in the door, your ability to connect, empathize, and engage with a team's values and culture is what sets you apart. Interviews—especially in the later stages—are your chance to demonstrate these essential qualities, turning formal evaluations into meaningful, dynamic conversations.

Building genuine rapport during an interview lays the groundwork for collaboration and teamwork. This is your moment to showcase

While your qualifications may get you in the door, your ability to connect, empathize, and engage with a team's values and culture is what sets you apart.

emotional intelligence through traits like empathy, self-awareness, and adaptability. Pay attention to nonverbal cues—like tone and body language—because they add depth to your communication. These subtle but powerful skills help build trust and turn interviews into two-way exchanges, making you more memorable and relatable.

Shift your mindset and approach interviews as dialogues, not just one-sided assessments. Prepare thoughtful questions that show your curiosity about the role and company culture and share stories that highlight your unique values and approach to problem-solving. By being authentic, you present not only your skills but also your mindset, personality, and approach to challenges.

Building these connections leaves a lasting impression, positioning you as a collaborative candidate eager to contribute meaningfully. Embracing this relational approach allows your enthusiasm and humanity to shine through, helping you stand out from the pack. Instead of being "just another candidate," you become a potential partner, excited to contribute to the team's success.

Actions to Elevate Your Interview Experience

▶ **Practice Active Listening and Reflective Responses:** Listen closely to your interviewer's words and respond thoughtfully. For instance, when they discuss a project, follow up with "That sounds fascinating—how did the team overcome those challenges, and what lessons did you take forward?" This demonstrates attentiveness and a genuine interest in their experience, creating a dialogue built on respect and engagement.

▶ **Prepare Thoughtful, Personalized Questions:** Research the company's mission and recent achievements to craft insightful questions. Instead of generic queries, delve deeper: "I saw your team recently launched an innovative campaign. How did you measure its success, and what insights did you gain?" These types of questions reflect your curiosity, preparation, and alignment with the company's goals.

▶ **Share Stories That Illustrate Your Strengths:** Bring your resume to life by sharing compelling stories. Instead of saying, "I managed a team," try "I led a team through a high-pressure project, assigning roles based on individual strengths and fostering open communication. We not only met the deadline but exceeded client expectations." These stories help interviewers visualize your contributions and see how you'd fit within their team.

Reflection Prompt

Think about one experience that defines your professional identity. How does it reflect your values and aspirations? Write it down and consider how you can share this story during a job interview or networking opportunity.

▶ **Exude Authentic Confidence:** Confidence is not about simply answering questions assertively; it's about owning your unique experiences and presenting them with pride. For example, "In my last role, I implemented a workflow that reduced errors by 20 percent, boosting efficiency and team morale." By highlighting your tangible impact, you project confidence, making a strong case for your candidacy.

▶ **Maintain a Positive Mindset:** Treat interviews as opportunities for growth, not high-stakes tests. Remember, you're evaluating the company as much as they are evaluating you. When discussing challenges, frame them as learning experiences: "I'm excited to tackle these obstacles— it's a great opportunity to apply my skills and learn from your team's approach." This mindset not only reduces interview anxiety but fosters authenticity, turning a high-pressure situation into a collaborative dialogue.

Why It Matters

Approaching interviews with emotional intelligence transforms them into meaningful exchanges. This mindset sets you apart as a candidate who values connection, collaboration, and growth. Employers will remember candidates who demonstrate these qualities, making you stand out in today's fast-paced hiring environment.

> **Step into your next interview with confidence, ready to connect authentically, share your story, and showcase your unique value.**

Step into your next interview with confidence, ready to connect authentically, share your story, and showcase your unique value. Meaningful professional relationships begin with genuine exchanges—and this is your moment to shine!

Strategy Two. Your Story Matters: Mastering the Art of Storytelling

Your personal story is a potent and transformative tool. It's more than just a collection of experiences—it's a vibrant reflection of how you face challenges, celebrate victories, and evolve. Each setback, every success, and all the lessons learned along the way have shaped you into the professional you are today. When you share your story with confidence, you turn your journey into an asset that resonates deeply with employers, giving you an edge in a competitive market.

Storytelling goes beyond effective communication—it is a bridge that builds **trust** and creates authentic **connections**. Employers aren't merely seeking qualifications; they want to understand the person behind the resume. By sharing your journey, you not only highlight your achievements but also reveal the values and growth that make you a unique asset to any team.

Your story isn't just a professional tool—it's a source of inspiration. By sharing your challenges and triumphs, you encourage others to reflect on their own journeys, fostering a culture of empathy and collaboration. Being open about setbacks shows they are part of growth, creating a work environment where authenticity and collective learning thrive.

As you prepare for interviews, crafting and presenting your story thoughtfully is essential. Tailor your narrative to the role, focusing on the experiences and skills that align with the position's requirements. This not only demonstrates your fit for the job but also conveys your passion and dedication, ensuring a lasting impression.

In today's world of impersonal interactions and fleeting connections, storytelling is what sets you apart.

In today's world of impersonal interactions and fleeting connections, storytelling is what sets you apart. It positions you as someone who values authenticity. Embrace your story—it is a vital part of your professional identity, showcasing your skills and character while guiding you toward fulfilling opportunities.

Actions to Share Your Story Effectively

▶ **Practice Telling Your Story:** Reflect on key milestones, challenges, and successes that highlight your skills and values. Rehearse presenting these moments, focusing on the lessons learned and their relevance to your career aspirations. Practicing builds confidence, ensuring you engage interviewers and leave a lasting impact.

▶ **Craft Your Resume as a Narrative:** Transform your resume into a cohesive story by adding context and quantifiable metrics. Instead of writing "Managed a marketing campaign," say, "Led a campaign that boosted traffic by 35 percent and generated $50,000 in revenue within three months." Quantifying your impact makes your contributions clear and compelling.

▶ **Expand Your Story in Your Cover Letter:** Your cover letter offers a chance to explore defining moments in your journey.

Share experiences that align with the company's mission, such as tackling a challenging project or solving a unique problem. These personal touches make your application more engaging and relatable.

▶ **Highlight Relevant Stories During Interviews:** Listen closely to interviewers and connect your experiences to their needs. For instance, if they discuss a team challenge, share a story about streamlining processes or solving a similar problem in a previous role. This tailored approach shows your readiness to contribute and your understanding of their objectives.

▶ **Express Passion and Alignment:** Demonstrate your enthusiasm by explaining how the company's values resonate with your own. If sustainability is a key focus, for example, share your experience leading a waste-reduction initiative. Genuine passion strengthens emotional connections and reinforces your alignment with their mission.

Your Story, Your Strength

Your career journey is a powerful narrative that connects your qualifications with your personal values and character. By crafting and sharing your story with pride, you position yourself as a well-rounded professional whose experiences align with the company's needs.

Remember, your story isn't just a collection of past events—it's a testament to your growth, resilience, and ambition. Share it confidently, and let it lead you to the success and fulfillment you deserve.

Strategy Three. Identifying Key Challenges: Articulating Your Problem-Solving Skills

Every role exists to address challenges and help the organization thrive. While thoughtful questions and charisma are important in interviews, showcasing your **problem-solving** abilities is essential. Employers seek candidates who can understand their obstacles and provide intelligent, tailored solutions.

> **While thoughtful questions and charisma are important in interviews, showcasing your problem-solving abilities is essential.**

Thorough preparation is crucial. Research the organization, its industry, and current trends. Explore its recent initiatives and challenges, such as customer satisfaction or innovation. Reflect on your past experiences where you've successfully handled similar challenges. By connecting these issues to your background, you position yourself as a proactive candidate ready to contribute.

In interviews, direct the conversation toward problem-solving. Ask insightful questions about the company's priorities to show your strategic mindset. For example, asking, "What are the top challenges this team faces?" highlights your genuine interest and sets you apart as someone eager to make an impact, not just fill a role.

Problem-solving is at the heart of most jobs. Whether it's improving efficiency, resolving conflicts, or driving innovation, your ability to tackle complex problems with creativity and focus makes you stand out. By aligning your background with their needs, you transition from a passive interviewee to an active participant in their success.

> **Problem-solving is at the heart of most jobs.**

Strategies for Highlighting Problem-Solving Skills

▶ **Prepare Detailed Problem-Solving Stories:** Identify past experiences where you overcame challenges. Use the **STAR method** (Situation, Task, Action, Result) to structure your story. For instance, explain how you reduced project delays by 30 percent through streamlined workflows, emphasizing your analytical skills and teamwork. Metrics and outcomes add credibility, making your story more compelling to interviewers.

▶ **Inquire About Company Challenges:** Ask targeted questions about the company's most pressing issues. For example, "What strategies has the team considered to address [specific challenge]?" This demonstrates your critical thinking and highlights your interest in the role, creating opportunities to relate your expertise to their needs.

▶ **Adopt a Problem-Solving Mindset:** Incorporate solutions-oriented language in your responses. Phrases like "I faced a similar challenge when..." connect your experiences to the company's needs. This shows your adaptability and resourcefulness, qualities highly valued in today's job market.

▶ **Showcase Collaborative Problem-Solving:** Describe instances where teamwork resolved significant challenges. For example, explain how leading cross-departmental meetings helped resolve conflicting priorities, improving processes and team morale. This highlights your ability to unite diverse perspectives to achieve shared goals.

▶ **Share Your Commitment to Improvement:** Employers value candidates who don't just solve problems but also prevent them. Share examples of when you identified root causes and implemented sustainable solutions. For instance, discuss a training program you introduced to reduce skill gaps, boosting team efficiency by 20 percent.

Aligning Your Story with Company Goals

Tailor your problem-solving examples to reflect the company's mission and challenges. Research their goals and demonstrate how your experiences align, positioning yourself as a confident problem-solver ready to integrate into their team. This proactive approach shows you're prepared to add immediate value.

Your problem-solving abilities reflect more than just professional expertise—they showcase resilience, creativity, and adaptability. By emphasizing these qualities, you position yourself as a candidate ready to lead and innovate.

By preparing thoughtfully, engaging strategically, and sharing your experiences compellingly, you transform problem-solving into a defining feature of your career narrative. Let your story shine and trust that your unique skills will guide you to opportunities aligned with your aspirations.

Strategy Four. Transforming Interviews into Impact: Crafting Meaningful Connections

Unlocking career potential means moving beyond simply presenting qualifications. In a competitive job market, it's essential to show how you can **integrate** into a team and contribute meaningfully to its goals. This approach transforms you from just another candidate into an indispensable asset for the organization.

Every job opening exists to address challenges and enhance success. Hiring managers seek candidates who understand the

> **Approach interviews as opportunities to position yourself as a problem-solver who aligns with the organization's needs.**

company's obstacles and provide actionable solutions. Approach interviews as opportunities to position yourself as a problem-solver who aligns with the organization's needs. This strategy not only highlights your readiness to grow but also conveys pride in seeking a workplace that values your contributions.

Strategies for Forging Genuine Connections

- ▶ **Practice Active Listening:** Active listening is essential for meaningful dialogue. Engage fully by focusing on the interviewer's words, maintaining eye contact, and responding thoughtfully. For instance, if they mention a challenge, respond with "That's interesting! How has the team approached this so far?" This fosters dynamic conversation, showing empathy, attentiveness, and enthusiasm for collaboration.
- ▶ **Prepare Insightful Questions About Team Dynamics:** Ask questions that reflect your interest in the company's culture and teamwork. For example, "How does your team ensure effective collaboration during high-pressure situations?" highlights your commitment to fostering communication and cohesion. These inquiries demonstrate that you're invested in contributing to a supportive work environment.
- ▶ **Share Specific Examples of Collaboration:** Stories of successful teamwork will make you stand out. For example: "In my last role, I co-led a cross-functional initiative to revamp our marketing strategy, ensuring input from every member. This approach resulted in a 25 percent increase in engagement metrics within three months." These examples illustrate your problem-solving skills and dedication to shared goals.
- ▶ **Express a Willingness to Learn from the Team:** Show humility and adaptability by emphasizing your readiness to grow

alongside colleagues. For example, ask, "What processes encourage knowledge sharing and mentorship within the team?" This signals your collaborative mindset and eagerness to learn from others' strengths.

▶ **Highlight the Importance of a Supportive Supervisor:** Your relationship with a supervisor greatly influences job satisfaction. Ask about their leadership style, for example, "How do you support team members in achieving their goals?" This demonstrates that you value a leader who fosters growth, aligning with your aspirations and highlighting your focus on constructive relationships.

Elevating Your Interview Approach

View interviews as more than just assessments—they're opportunities to demonstrate your character, values, and commitment to team success. Approach these interactions with authenticity, confidence, and curiosity. Showcase how your unique skills align with the organization's vision and demonstrate your dedication to collaboration.

> **View interviews as more than just assessments— they're opportunities to demonstrate your character, values, and commitment to team success.**

By focusing on genuine connections, you increase your chances of securing the role and position yourself as a valuable, engaged team member. Let your story and achievements reflect your pride and readiness to make a meaningful impact in any professional setting.

Strategy Five. Creating Enthusiasm: Building Rapport in Interviews

Humans naturally gravitate toward those who radiate **enthusiasm** and share their passions authentically. I've often been told, "I love your energy!"—and that energy is powerful. Demonstrating genuine excitement for your work—whether it's a project, a cause, or your craft—does more than highlight your expertise. It fosters engagement, collaboration, and inspiration.

As you prepare for interviews, remember that your enthusiasm is your superpower. Sharing it authentically leaves a lasting impression, setting you apart as someone who is not only skilled but driven. By letting your passion shine, you create deep connections that open doors to meaningful opportunities.

> **As you prepare for interviews, remember that your enthusiasm is your superpower.**

The Power of Passion in Interviews

Entering an interview with enthusiasm does more than convey qualifications—it shows hiring managers you're genuinely invested in the role and the company. Your energy sets the tone, inviting them to imagine how your spirit can elevate the team. Hiring decisions often weigh cultural alignment and positive energy alongside technical skills. When your enthusiasm aligns with the company's mission, you stand out as a candidate eager to inspire and add value.

Articulating your passion effectively requires focus. Highlight specific aspects of the role or organization that excite you. Are you inspired by their innovative approach, sustainability efforts, or collaborative culture? Sharing your motivations paints a compelling picture of your alignment with their goals, positioning you as a meaningful contributor.

Enthusiasm is also infectious. When you express genuine passion, you energize the conversation, transforming the interview into a dynamic dialogue. This approach makes the experience more memorable and enjoyable, leaving a stronger impression than candidates who focus solely on technical details.

Strategies for Showcasing Enthusiasm

- ▶ **Start with a Personal Story:** Share an anecdote that illustrates your passion and adds a personal touch:
  - ★ *"From a young age, I've loved solving complex puzzles, which led me to a career in software engineering. I find satisfaction in breaking down challenges and seeing results come to life—like when I led a team to develop an app that boosted user engagement by 30 percent."*
  - ★ Such stories make your passion tangible and relatable.
- ▶ **Ask Passion-Driven Questions:** Frame your questions around shared values to demonstrate genuine interest:
  - ★ *"I read about your efforts to reduce environmental impact through sustainable manufacturing. How has that initiative evolved, and what role does the team play in its success?"*
  - ★ This shows you've done your research and that your passion aligns with their objectives.
- ▶ **Express Enthusiasm for Team Culture:** Highlight your excitement for collaboration and a dynamic workplace:
  - ★ *"I'm excited about joining a team that values collaboration as much as innovation. Could you share how team members foster creativity on complex projects?"*
  - ★ This conveys your eagerness to contribute to a positive, productive environment.

Elevating Your Interview Experience

Interviews are more than evaluations—they're opportunities to showcase your authentic self and build meaningful connections. Your passion is an essential part of your professional identity. Expressing it confidently can set the stage for collaborative, fulfilling work relationships.

By preparing thoughtful questions, sharing engaging stories, and exuding enthusiasm, you create a memorable interview experience. This approach reinforces your qualifications while demonstrating genuine care for the role and the company's success.

Let your passion unlock new opportunities. Approach each interview as a chance to connect, inspire, and contribute. Your enthusiasm can light the way to a career that aligns with your aspirations and potential!

INSIGHTS TO MASTER STORYTELLING FOR CAREER SUCCESS

Storytelling is a bridge that fosters empathy, understanding, and trust.

Storytelling Builds Connection

When you share your journey authentically, you invite others to relate to your experiences and values. This connection builds the foundation for meaningful collaboration and establishes you as someone who inspires and unites. Moreover, storytelling enables you to leave a lasting emotional impact, transforming professional interactions into memorable experiences.

Your Narrative Reflects Your Values

Every story you tell reveals the principles and priorities that shape your character. Sharing lessons from challenges and triumphs showcases your integrity, perseverance, and passion. This alignment between your values and professional goals makes you a compelling and credible candidate. By highlighting the values that define you, your story becomes a guidepost for both personal and professional relationships, creating alignment and fostering trust.

Storytelling Showcases Problem-Solving

Stories of adversity highlight your ability to navigate complex challenges and deliver impactful solutions. Framing these experiences in real-world contexts demonstrates your critical thinking and adaptability, positioning you as a resourceful and innovative problem-solver. These stories also signal your ability to anticipate future challenges and proactively contribute to the success of any organization.

Personal Stories Make You Memorable

Facts and figures can blend into the background, but a well-told story leaves a lasting impression. Sharing personal anecdotes adds depth and relatability to your profile, making you stand out as a dynamic, memorable candidate. Your ability to captivate with a story not only distinguishes you but also ensures that your narrative resonates long after the conversation ends, reinforcing your unique value.

Stories Foster Growth and Inspiration

By sharing your journey, you inspire reflection and growth in others. Your openness about successes and setbacks fosters a culture of authenticity and collaboration, creating professional environments where shared success and mutual support thrive. Each story you tell has the potential to spark innovative ideas and strengthen connections, amplifying your impact beyond the immediate interaction.

YOUR NEXT STEPS: CRAFTING YOUR UNIQUE STORY

Storytelling is a transformative skill that helps you connect, inspire, and stand out in a competitive job market. Now that you've explored how to harness this power, it's time to put it into action. These steps will guide you in crafting and sharing your narrative effectively, enabling you to create meaningful connections and amplify your professional impact.

1. Craft Your Defining Story

Identify the experiences that define your professional identity and reflect your core values.

- ▶ Think of a significant moment in your career or personal life where you overcame a challenge or achieved something meaningful.
- ▶ Reflect on the skills and values that helped you navigate the situation and the lessons you learned.

Action Step: Write a one-paragraph version of this story, focusing on how it showcases your character, skills, and growth. Practice sharing it confidently in conversations or interviews.

2. Connect Your Story to Employer Needs

Align your narrative with the goals and challenges of prospective employers.

- Research the company or industry to understand its priorities and potential challenges.
- Select a personal or professional story that illustrates how your background aligns with their needs.

Action Step: Prepare to share your story during interviews or networking events, emphasizing how your experience equips you to contribute to their mission.

3. Refine Your Storytelling Skills

Develop your ability to engage and inspire through storytelling.

- Practice telling your story out loud, focusing on clarity, emotional resonance, and pacing.
- Seek feedback from trusted colleagues or mentors to enhance your delivery.

Action Step: Record yourself telling a story and review it to identify areas for improvement. Refine your tone, body language, and emphasis to create a compelling narrative.

4. Use Storytelling to Strengthen Connections

Build trust and rapport by sharing authentic stories in professional settings.

- Identify opportunities to incorporate storytelling into your interactions, such as interviews, meetings, or presentations.

> ▶ Share a story that reflects your ability to collaborate, problem-solve, or adapt to new challenges.

Action Step: During your next professional interaction, intentionally share a story that aligns with the conversation, highlighting your values and strengths.

5. Build a Portfolio of Stories

Create a library of narratives that highlight different aspects of your experience and skills.

> ▶ Compile three to five key stories that showcase your problem-solving abilities, leadership qualities, or significant achievements.
> ▶ Tailor each story for different audiences, ensuring they align with specific roles or industries.

Action Step: Write brief summaries of each story and note the skills or lessons they emphasize. Use this portfolio as a resource for interviews, networking, or personal branding.

YOUR STORY, YOUR SUPERPOWER

Storytelling is more than a professional tool—it's an expression of who you are and the value you bring to the world. By honing your narrative, aligning it with your aspirations, and sharing it authentically, you create opportunities to connect, inspire, and thrive.

Trust in the power of your experiences, and let your story be the key that opens doors to meaningful relationships and career success. Every story you tell has the potential to make an impact—start sharing yours today!

Trust in the power of your experiences, and let your story be the key that opens doors to meaningful relationships and career success.

Treat your reputation as the invaluable asset it is. Let it guide you toward success, and let that success inspire others to follow.

CHAPTER 4

FUTURE-PROOFING YOUR CAREER

Building Resilience for Long-Term Success

Change is inevitable, and in today's rapidly shifting professional landscape, embracing it is not just a necessity but an opportunity to grow and thrive. The journey to **future-proofing** your career begins with a commitment to learning, adapting, and aligning your skills with the demands of an ever-evolving world. This isn't simply about keeping up—it's about standing out.

This is the essence of future-proofing: transforming uncertainty into possibility and equipping yourself with the tools to thrive in a dynamic environment.

Picture yourself as an architect of your career, designing a path that not only withstands the tests of time but flourishes in the face of challenges. Each step forward, each skill you acquire, and each lesson learned add to the structure of a fulfilling and resilient professional life. This is the essence of future-proofing: transforming uncertainty into possibility and equipping yourself with the tools to thrive in a dynamic environment.

It all starts with mindset. Adopting a lifelong learner mentality unlocks doors you never thought possible. Think of change not as a disruption but as a catalyst for discovery. With curiosity as your compass, every technological advancement, market shift, or industry trend becomes an opportunity to innovate and grow. Enrolling in a course, reading a thought-provoking article, or exploring a new digital tool isn't just about gaining knowledge—it's about embracing the pride of knowing you're investing in yourself and your potential.

Imagine approaching the job market not with hesitation but with confidence, knowing your skills are sharp and your adaptability is unmatched. See yourself not merely as a participant in your industry but as an innovator shaping its future. This transformation begins when you decide to align your actions with your aspirations, making intentional choices to fuel your growth.

Future-proofing is not just about career security; it's about fulfillment. It's about finding joy in discovery, purpose in progress, and pride in the contributions you bring to your field. By embracing continuous learning, you create a narrative of resilience and relevance that speaks louder than any resume.

> **By embracing continuous learning, you create a narrative of resilience and relevance that speaks louder than any resume.**

This chapter is your guide to crafting that narrative. Together, we'll explore strategies to identify skills that matter, nurture them with intention, and communicate them with pride. You'll discover how to navigate challenges with confidence and turn them into stepping stones toward a more enriched and impactful career.

REFLECTION MOMENT

Before diving into the fundamentals, let's take a moment to reflect on where you are and where you want to go. Use these prompts to ground yourself and ignite your curiosity:

1. **Identifying Your Aspirations:** Think about a time when you felt truly energized and fulfilled by your work. What skills were you using, and how did they contribute to your success?
2. **Embracing the Future:** Consider an area of knowledge or a skill you've been meaning to explore. How could mastering it transform your career trajectory?
3. **Taking the First Step:** Write down three small actions you could take this week to start building a new skill or deepening your expertise.

Reflect on these questions and let them guide you as we move into the fundamentals of lifelong learning and adaptability. Your future is waiting—it's time to seize it with pride, purpose, and determination.

Let's begin this journey together, building the foundation for a career that not only endures but thrives.

CULTIVATE LIFELONG LEARNING: FIVE FUNDAMENTALS FOR ADAPTABILITY AND GROWTH

Adaptability and a willingness to learn can propel your career. Follow these five steps to foster lifelong learning.

Fundamental One. Maximize Your LinkedIn Impact: Elevate Your Career Through Connection

LinkedIn is more than just a platform; it's your digital stage for building meaningful connections, showcasing your expertise, and future-proofing your career in today's competitive job market. In an era where a professional online presence is nonnegotiable, skipping LinkedIn could mean missing out on visibility and opportunities. By embracing its potential, you position yourself to stand out and resonate with employers, collaborators, and industry peers.

Think of your LinkedIn profile as a living, breathing **highlight reel** of your professional journey. It's your digital elevator pitch—a curated space to reflect your qualifications, aspirations, and personal brand. Rather than simply listing roles and achievements, craft a narrative that tells your story. Start with a professional yet personable headline, a compelling summary that shares your mission, and detailed experiences that emphasize measurable accomplishments.

> **The magic of LinkedIn isn't just in creating a profile—it's in how you engage with the platform.**

The magic of LinkedIn isn't just in creating a profile—it's in how you engage with the platform. Sharing insights through posts, publishing articles, and joining discussions enhances your visibility and strengthens your professional credibility. Each interaction builds a content-rich history, positioning you as a thought leader in your field. The goal? Be active, influential, and consistently valuable to your network.

While the term "personal branding" may seem overused, its importance is undeniable. Your brand is how you communicate your unique value. Activities like sharing industry insights, commenting on trends, or even hosting webinars reinforce your expertise. This visibility elevates your reputation and opens doors for new collaborations, connections, and career growth.

As the co-founder of a retail recruiting company, I've witnessed the transformative power of a robust LinkedIn presence. Unfortunately, many professionals underutilize this platform, missing valuable opportunities to connect with recruiters and showcase their potential. This is a missed chance, as LinkedIn provides a dynamic view of candidates, emphasizing skills, accomplishments, and personality—qualities that go beyond traditional resumes.

Optimizing your LinkedIn profile begins with a strong foundation:

- ▶ Use a professional photo.
- ▶ Craft a headline that's both concise and impactful.
- ▶ Write a summary that highlights your goals and achievements with clarity and enthusiasm.

Include quantifiable accomplishments in your experience section, request endorsements and recommendations, and integrate media like articles, portfolios, or project links to make your profile visually engaging.

Networking is just as critical as profile optimization. Focus on quality over quantity—connect thoughtfully with professionals in your industry and beyond. Personalize your connection requests and nurture relationships by engaging with your network's content. Even second-degree connections can lead to unexpected opportunities, providing referrals or insights that significantly enhance your prospects.

Stay active to amplify your visibility. Post regularly, share industry insights, and engage with discussions in relevant groups. Use features like "Open to Work" and tailored job alerts to signal your readiness for new opportunities. LinkedIn's algorithms reward consistent engagement, ensuring your profile stays discoverable to recruiters and hiring managers.

LinkedIn isn't just a tool—it's a career development powerhouse. By cultivating a dynamic presence, you present yourself as a standout candidate and craft a narrative that resonates across industries. Every post, interaction, and update reinforces your personal brand, showcasing the unique human pride and potential you bring to any role.

So take charge of your LinkedIn journey today. Build a profile that reflects your passion, create authentic connections, and engage meaningfully within your industry. The effort you put in now will open doors, foster meaningful relationships, and propel your career toward the success you envision.

Start today. Elevate your LinkedIn presence and watch as your opportunities and network grow exponentially.

Start today. Elevate your LinkedIn presence and watch as your opportunities and network grow exponentially.

Fundamental Two. Build Your Advisory Board: Harness Mentorship for Career Empowerment

Imagine navigating your career with a team of trusted guides offering invaluable insights at every critical juncture. In *Retail Pride*, I introduced the transformative idea of creating a **personal advisory board**—a concept that has only grown more impactful over time.

Think of this board as a curated circle of mentors: seasoned professionals who bring diverse expertise, strategic foresight, and meaningful guidance to help you tackle challenges, seize opportunities, and confidently chart your path.

An advisory board does more than offer advice—it enhances your decision-making, expands your perspective, and nurtures your potential. By surrounding yourself with individuals from different backgrounds and industries, you gain access to unique viewpoints that challenge and inspire you. This network becomes your compass, helping you navigate complex decisions and motivating you to dream bigger.

Curating Your Advisory Board

Building an advisory board starts with identifying people whose experiences resonate with your goals and values. Look beyond your immediate field—diversity in expertise fosters richer insights. Reach out respectfully, using

Building an advisory board starts with identifying people whose experiences resonate with your goals and values.

platforms like LinkedIn or through mutual connections. Don't underestimate the power of asking; many successful individuals are eager to share their knowledge when approached with sincerity. Engage them in meaningful conversations, demonstrate genuine curiosity about their journeys, and ask thoughtful questions that spark deep dialogue.

Practical Steps to Create Your Advisory Board

> ▶ **Identify Potential Advisors:** Seek individuals who embody the qualities you aspire to develop—leaders in your industry, insightful colleagues, or even trusted friends. A diverse

board ensures broader perspectives and more robust decision-making.

- ▶ **Approach Thoughtfully:** When reaching out, express genuine interest in their experiences and articulate how their guidance could support your growth. A respectful, curiosity-driven approach sets the stage for a productive exchange.
- ▶ **Ask Meaningful Questions:** Prepare questions that invite rich conversations and reflect your commitment to growth. Examples include:
  - ★ How do you see my strengths aligning with my aspirations?
  - ★ What advice would you offer as I pursue my passions?
  - ★ Are there unexplored areas I should consider to maximize my potential?
  - ★ How can I evolve to better align with my goals?

Making Your Advisory Board Dynamic

An advisory board isn't static—it's a living, evolving network. Regularly check in to share updates, seek guidance, and explore new challenges. This consistent engagement fosters trust, strengthens relationships, and ensures your career remains aligned with your aspirations.

When someone asks me to mentor them, I often suggest, "Let me be part of your advisory board. Share who else you've included, and let's collaborate." This approach shifts mentorship from a one-on-one dynamic to a collective effort, enriching the experience for everyone involved.

The Broader Impact of Mentorship

Your advisory board isn't just about professional guidance—it's about building a community that inspires and uplifts you. These conversations enhance self-awareness, fuel growth, and celebrate your achievements. In embracing this process, you create a network that supports your vision and drives you toward extraordinary success.

Reflection Prompt

Think of three individuals in your professional circle who could provide valuable guidance. What steps can you take to strengthen these relationships? Reach out this week with a thoughtful question or shared resource to foster deeper connection.

Taking the First Step

Start building your advisory board today. Reach out, engage, and nurture relationships that will transform your career and life. This team of mentors is more than a support system—it's a catalyst for growth, resilience, and extraordinary success. Together, you and your advisors can achieve remarkable things!

Fundamental Three. Unlock the Treasure of Knowledge: How Cross-Training Fuels Career Longevity

In today's fast-paced job market, adaptability and growth aren't just advantages—they're the keys to unlocking a thriving future. By embracing continuous learning, you remain competitive, ready to seize opportunities that propel your career forward.

One of the most transformative strategies to future-proof your career is cross-training: deliberately expanding your skillset beyond your primary responsibilities.

One of the most transformative strategies to future-proof your career is **cross-training**: deliberately expanding your skillset beyond your primary responsibilities. In industries like retail, cross-training fosters agility, enabling team members to take on multiple roles, improve collaboration, and drive efficiency. Those who embrace this practice become irreplaceable problem-solvers, ready to tackle challenges and deliver unexpected value. Resilience becomes second nature, benefitting both individuals and their teams.

Beyond the Workplace: A Personal Revolution

Cross-training isn't limited to immediate job benefits—it's a powerful tool for personal development. By diving into skills and knowledge from diverse fields, you cultivate adaptability, innovation, and a growth mindset—traits that guarantee success in any industry.

What if your career wasn't confined to a single path but was a dynamic evolution, embracing multiple disciplines and perspectives? Imagine a marketer applying psychological insights or a technologist inspired by design principles. Cross-disciplinary learning doesn't just open doors; it unlocks worlds of opportunity, creativity, and collaboration.

Why Cross-Disciplinary Learning Matters

- ► **Broaden Your Perspectives:** Explore new fields to uncover creative solutions and tackle challenges with confidence. For instance, sustainability can influence business strategies, while leadership theories transform team dynamics.
- ► **Ignite Creativity:** Diverse disciplines inspire fresh ideas. A manager may apply artistic techniques to presentations, or a biologist might revolutionize product design.
- ► **Build Versatile Skills:** Skills like coding, design thinking, or project management make you a sought-after asset, ready to excel across industries.

- **Enhance Collaboration:** Understanding varied disciplines fosters mutual respect and deeper teamwork, driving groundbreaking innovation.
- **Be Ready for Change:** A broad skillset allows you to pivot seamlessly, adapting to disruptions and embracing new opportunities.
- **Fuel Lifelong Learning:** Curiosity drives continuous growth, keeping you adaptable and forward-thinking.

Starting Your Cross-Training Journey

Begin small, exploring areas that spark your interest. Dive into an online course, attend a workshop, or join a professional network. Are you in finance? Learn data visualization to enrich your reports. A writer? Explore coding to create immersive content. Each new skill adds depth to your expertise and boosts your ability to connect ideas from different fields.

This journey isn't just about learning—it's about becoming an innovator. The ability to integrate knowledge from diverse domains sets you apart as a creative problem-solver.

This is more than career survival—it's about shaping a professional life filled with purpose, growth, and fulfillment.

The Transformative Power of Cross-Training

Every new discipline you master builds not only your skills but also your confidence. Cross-training strengthens your intellectual agility, positioning you as a resilient leader ready to navigate the challenges of tomorrow.

This is more than career survival—it's about shaping a professional life filled with purpose, growth, and fulfillment.

Your Journey Starts Now

Don't wait. Start today. Let cross-training inspire you to explore, learn, and grow into the innovative professional you're destined to be. Watch as your career evolves, fueled by creativity, adaptability, and a passion for lifelong discovery.

Take the first step—and let your journey lead to unparalleled success!

Fundamental Four. Create a Legacy of Excellence: The Power of Reputation in Your Career

In today's highly competitive world, your **reputation** isn't just a reflection of what you've done—it's the foundation for what you'll achieve in the future. It's more than a collection of past accolades; it's the perception others have of your reliability, integrity, and value. In a dynamic, multigenerational workforce, where collaboration and trust are paramount, your reputation plays an essential role in your career growth and the lasting impact you can make.

> **Consistently delivering excellence builds credibility, earns respect, and drives career advancement—transforming you from just another professional into someone who makes an indelible mark.**

Think of your reputation as your professional currency—it opens doors, earns trust, and ensures you're remembered for the right reasons. While your skills may get you noticed, your reputation secures the trust and relationships that will carry you forward. Consistently delivering excellence builds credibility, earns respect, and drives career advancement—transforming you from just another professional into someone who makes an indelible mark.

The Building Blocks of a Strong Reputation

Developing a strong reputation is crucial for advancing your career, and it begins with several key building blocks.

Commitment to Excellence

This commitment isn't limited to the work itself; it's reflected in your attitude toward your profession. Embrace feedback, strive for improvement, and exceed expectations—all these actions contribute to a legacy of reliability and achievement that others can depend on.

Professionalism and Integrity

Professionalism isn't just how you dress or speak; it's about how you interact with others and how you approach challenges. Respectful communication, active listening, and a positive attitude foster collaboration and trust. Integrity elevates these actions, ensuring your behavior aligns with your values. Admitting mistakes, maintaining transparency, and honoring commitments demonstrate accountability and strengthen relationships. This foundation is the bedrock of a reputation that stands the test of time.

The Role of Your Personal Brand

Your reputation is the essence of your personal brand. It's a blend of your skills, character, and the ability to inspire others. Thoughtfully cultivating your personal brand through networking, engaging communication, and maintaining a strong online presence enhances your visibility. Sharing expertise on platforms like LinkedIn or contributing to industry events reinforces your identity as a reliable, forward-thinking professional that others want to work with.

The Power of Word of Mouth

In today's connected world, word of mouth is invaluable. A strong reputation makes your name synonymous with trustworthiness and excellence. Colleagues, clients, and partners who speak highly of you can open doors to new roles or projects that you may not have sought out on your own. Your reputation is a form of social proof, validating your skills and character alongside your expertise.

Your Legacy of Excellence

A reputation for excellence is far more than a career asset—it's an investment in your future. By consistently maintaining high standards, you not only advance your own career, but you also inspire others to do the same. This ripple effect elevates teams and organizations, creating a culture of excellence where everyone strives for higher achievements.

Practical Steps to Build and Protect Your Reputation

- **Deliver Consistently:** Every task is an opportunity to exceed expectations and reinforce trust and reliability.
- **Cultivate Relationships:** Build meaningful connections with clear communication, empathy, and collaboration at the core.
- **Seek Feedback:** Actively ask for input to identify areas for growth and demonstrate your commitment to continuous improvement.
- **Express Gratitude:** Recognize and celebrate others' contributions, fostering a positive, supportive environment that benefits everyone.
- **Maintain Integrity:** Be honest, transparent, and accountable, ensuring that your actions always reflect ethical standards and personal pride.

Your Reputation: A Legacy of Pride

Your professional reputation is a reflection of the pride and passion you bring to your work. By committing to excellence, nurturing relationships, and upholding integrity, you build a legacy that enhances your career and inspires those around you.

Now is the time to reflect—what story does your reputation tell? Does it showcase resilience, collaboration, and impact? If so, you're already shaping a legacy that will be felt for years to come. Treat your reputation as the invaluable asset it is. Let it guide you toward success, and let that success inspire others to follow.

Treat your reputation as the invaluable asset it is. Let it guide you toward success, and let that success inspire others to follow.

Take pride in your reputation—it's the foundation of everything to come.

Fundamental Five. Embrace a Learning Mindset: Shape Your Evolving Professional Path

Picture your career as a journey—each experience building upon the last, refining your skills, and opening new doors. In today's fast-paced world, cultivating a **learning mindset** isn't just important—it's essential. Curiosity, agility, and adaptability are your tickets to thriving in uncertainty. These qualities turn every moment into an opportunity for growth and transformation.

Transforming Challenges into Opportunities

When challenges arise, embrace them as opportunities for growth rather than obstacles. Shift your mindset to see setbacks as chances to stretch your abilities and build resilience. Stepping outside your comfort zone or taking on a new challenge isn't just a test—it's a learning experience that sharpens your skills and reveals new possibilities.

By approaching challenges with a willingness to learn, you turn them into stepping stones toward transformation. This mindset builds confidence and resilience, two qualities essential for navigating today's complex and ever-changing workplace.

The Power of Agility and Reflection

A learning mindset goes hand-in-hand with **agility**—the ability to pivot and adapt to change. Whether you're diving into a cross-functional project or embracing a new industry trend, agility ensures that you're always growing, innovating, and collaborating.

Equally important is the power of **reflection**. Pausing to assess the lessons from both your successes and setbacks helps you uncover patterns and insights that guide your future decisions. Each moment of introspection turns experience into actionable knowledge, giving you the clarity to move forward with intention.

Embracing a learning mindset isn't just a personal growth tool—it's a professional asset.

Showcasing Your Learning Mindset

Embracing a learning mindset isn't just a personal growth tool—it's a professional asset. During interviews or networking conversations, share stories that highlight your growth and adaptability. For example, recount a time when you turned a failed project into a success by learning from mistakes and adjusting your approach. These stories demonstrate your problem-solving skills and your commitment to growth—traits that employers value deeply.

Sharing your learning journey also fosters connection. It shows you're collaborative, open-minded, and focused not only on your success but also on uplifting your team and your organization. This willingness to learn signals that you're ready to contribute and grow within any team, making you a standout candidate.

Crafting a Career of Continuous Growth

Your career is a living narrative—a story of evolution, resilience, and accomplishment. A learning mindset ensures that this story remains vibrant, enriched by each new experience. Every new role, every challenge overcome, and every piece of feedback adds a layer of depth and insight to your professional journey.

Your career is a living narrative—a story of evolution, resilience, and accomplishment.

Think about how your career has evolved. What lessons have challenges taught you? How have your skills and values shifted over time? By refining your approach continually, you ensure your career remains aligned with your aspirations and relevant to the world around you.

Reflection Prompt

Recall a time in your career when unexpected change challenged you. How did you adapt, and what did you learn from that experience? Reflect on how this skill prepares you for the challenges ahead.

Actions to Cultivate a Learning Mindset

- ▶ **Pursue New Experiences:** Take on roles or projects that stretch your abilities, expand your skills, and broaden your perspective.
- ▶ **Reflect Regularly:** Take time to assess your achievements and setbacks, turning them into actionable insights for future success.
- ▶ **Engage in Lifelong Learning:** Continuously explore new topics through courses, workshops, or mentorships to stay curious and relevant.
- ▶ **Welcome Feedback:** See feedback as an opportunity to refine your approach, enhance effectiveness, and become even better at what you do.
- ▶ **Set Dynamic Goals:** Align your career objectives with opportunities for growth, ensuring your aspirations remain exciting and purpose-driven.

The Journey Ahead

Every experience you encounter—whether triumphant or challenging—enriches your professional story. A learning mindset allows you to thrive amid change, unlocking new opportunities and creating meaningful contributions along the way.

Let your commitment to growth inspire not only yourself but also those around you. Cultivate curiosity, collaboration, and excellence in everything you do. Your career isn't just a destination—it's an ever-evolving adventure filled with purpose and potential.

Step boldly into the unknown, knowing you have the ability to adapt, learn, and flourish. This mindset will sustain your success and enrich your fulfillment, making your journey as rewarding as it is transformative.

ESSENTIAL TAKEAWAYS FOR BUILDING RESILIENCE

The cornerstone of future-proofing your career begins with adopting a mindset of continuous growth and discovery.

Adopt a Continuous Learning Mindset

In a world where change is the only constant, staying relevant means proactively updating your skillset and seeking out new challenges. Every experience—whether a success or setback— becomes a stepping stone that hones your abilities and deepens your understanding. Embrace curiosity and adaptability as the driving forces behind your journey, knowing that each challenge is an opportunity to expand your expertise and emerge stronger. By doing this, you don't just survive change—you thrive in it, positioning yourself as a resilient professional who embraces progress with open arms.

Embrace Adaptability as a Strength

In today's fast-paced, ever-evolving job market, adaptability is not just a skill—it's a superpower. Your ability to pivot, take on new responsibilities, and embrace fresh opportunities reflects resilience and a forward-thinking mindset. This flexibility ensures that you aren't just reacting to change—you are shaping your path and making each challenge work for you. Employers seek individuals who can not only integrate seamlessly into evolving environments but also offer innovative solutions and an open mind. This adaptability makes you a true asset, one who can lead and adapt no matter the circumstances.

Build and Leverage a Strong Professional Network

Meaningful relationships build your career. Surrounding yourself with mentors, peers, and thought leaders ignites collaboration, sparks creativity, and opens doors to new opportunities. Platforms like LinkedIn are more than just digital profiles—they are the gateways to your professional community. By nurturing authentic relationships and engaging actively, you create a network of support that propels you forward and elevates both your professional and personal growth. The stronger your network, the greater your influence—and the more you can contribute to the success of others.

Invest in Cross-Training and Multidisciplinary Learning

Don't just settle for mastering one set of skills—expand your horizons by cross-training and exploring multiple disciplines. This not only enhances your versatility but positions you as a multifaceted professional capable of adapting to a variety of challenges. Cross-training equips you with the tools to collaborate effectively across teams, while diving into new fields—whether through workshops, courses, or hands-on projects—sparks creativity and innovative problem-solving. Embrace the beauty of a holistic learning approach, where each new skill you acquire is a puzzle piece that strengthens your value and prepares you for the dynamic landscape ahead.

Prioritize Your Reputation as a
Professional Asset

Your reputation is your most valuable asset in the workplace—it's the currency that opens doors, builds trust, and sets the foundation for lasting relationships. Your work ethic, integrity, and professionalism shape how others see you. Consistency is key—by delivering excellence, maintaining high ethical standards, and fostering positive relationships, you build a reputation that goes beyond a job title. This legacy of respect and trust allows you to make a lasting impact, not only in your field but also in the lives of those around you. Guard your reputation with pride—it is your legacy in the making.

YOUR NEXT STEPS:
TAKING CHARGE OF YOUR FUTURE

Congratulations on completing the first part of the book! You've equipped yourself with the strategies to shape a resilient, future-proofed career. Now it's time to take action and bring your insights to life. Every step you take toward growth and progress is a commitment to owning your future. Pride in your journey begins with taking the next step with intention and confidence. Let's dive in.

1. Expand Your Expertise

Embrace lifelong learning and commit to mastering a skill that excites you. This is your chance to empower yourself for the future.

- ▷ Choose one skill or topic you're passionate about—whether it's data analytics, public speaking, or learning a new language.
- ▷ Find courses, workshops, or resources on platforms like Coursera, LinkedIn Learning, or industry webinars that align with your goals.

▶ Set a timeline and dedicate consistent time to this pursuit. Even thirty minutes a day adds up, fueling your growth and resilience.

Pro Tip: Share your journey on LinkedIn or with colleagues to stay accountable and inspire others to embrace continuous growth.

2. Assemble Your Personal Board of Advisors

You don't have to navigate your career alone. Build your network of trusted guides to help you accelerate your growth.

▶ Think about the people whose insights have inspired you and aim for a mix of mentors, peers, and industry leaders who can offer different perspectives.

▶ Create a list of at least five potential advisors and reach out to one this month. Be specific about what you hope to learn and show genuine appreciation for their time.

▶ Prepare thoughtful questions, like:
  ★ What challenges have shaped your career the most?
  ★ How would you approach the challenges I'm currently facing?
  ★ What growth areas would you recommend for someone in my position?

Pro Tip: Keep in touch and update your advisors on your progress. These relationships thrive on mutual engagement and trust.

3. Supercharge Your LinkedIn Presence

LinkedIn is a powerful platform to showcase your professional brand and amplify your visibility. Take charge of your digital presence today!

- Spend thirty minutes this week to refresh your profile—highlight recent accomplishments, ensure your summary reflects your aspirations, and update relevant skills and certifications.
- Engage with your network by posting insightful articles, joining professional discussions, or participating in industry-specific groups.
- Use features like Open to Work, tailored job alerts, and endorsements to amplify your visibility and connect with potential opportunities.

Pro Tip: Consistency is key—schedule regular updates to keep your profile relevant and your network engaged.

YOUR CAREER, YOUR STORY

These actions are more than just tasks—they are the building blocks of your career evolution. By committing to continuous learning, fostering meaningful connections, and creating a standout digital presence, you're not just future-proofing your career—you're shaping a path filled with growth, opportunity, and fulfillment.

> **These actions are more than just tasks—they are the building blocks of your career evolution.**

Take the first step today. The future you're building starts now! Own your journey and step boldly into the career you deserve.

PART 2

FOR THE LEADER

Human Pride Is a Leader's Greatest Resource

One vital lesson: transparency and continuous learning don't weaken authority—they strengthen it.

CHAPTER 5

UNLOCKING THE POTENTIAL OF HUMAN PRIDE

The heartbeat of every successful organization is its people. It's not just about the skills, the credentials, or the training—they are important, but what truly drives extraordinary outcomes is human pride. The pride employees take in their work—their sense of connection, value, and purpose—fuels their performance as well as the entire workplace culture.

HOW PRIDE DRIVES ENGAGEMENT, RETENTION, AND EXCELLENCE

When pride is ignited, it unlocks commitment, motivation, and dedication, creating an environment where everyone feels their contribution matters. Pride is the catalyst for engagement, retention, and excellence.

Pride is the catalyst for engagement, retention, and excellence.

Imagine a team where every person feels valued, seen, and celebrated. Pride nurtures this environment, transforming a workplace into a place where passion, creativity, and collaboration thrive. Leaders who acknowledge and nurture pride—recognizing not just achievements but the effort, resilience, and dedication to them—create a workplace where success is measured not only by metrics but by growth and fulfillment.

When employees feel proud of their work, they begin to see themselves as indispensable, and this feeling propels them to take on challenges with renewed confidence. They start pushing boundaries and uncovering their hidden potential. Pride fuels innovation and excellence, creating a vibrant, thriving work environment that encourages everyone to reach their fullest potential.

HUMAN PRIDE: THE MISSING INGREDIENT IN MODERN LEADERSHIP

In today's digital age, the nature of work is shifting. Leaders face a unique challenge: to inspire pride and purpose in teams that may feel disconnected or disengaged. Yet, when you tap into the power of pride, you create an environment where people are eager to contribute, collaborate, and excel.

> **The key question leaders must ask themselves regularly is "How proud are my team members of their work?"**

The key question leaders must ask themselves regularly is "How proud are my team members of their work?" The answers to this question will dictate the level of engagement and performance in the workplace. When you foster pride, your team becomes more than a group of employees—it becomes a cohesive unit, bonded by shared values and mutual respect. This pride-driven engagement elevates performance, reduces turnover, and inspires sustained success.

MY JOURNEY IN CULTIVATING HUMAN PRIDE

As I reflect on my leadership journey, the importance of pride is clear. In the early stages of my career, I noticed the most successful teams were those whose members took genuine pride in their work. It was not just about meeting targets; it was about creating an environment where employees felt respected and valued. This realization ignited my mission to build workplaces that celebrated pride—not just as an outcome but as an ongoing motivator.

When I implemented recognition programs early in my career, I saw firsthand how pride could transform a team's performance. These initiatives weren't based solely on numbers—they recognized resilience, effort, and personal growth. As a result, teams exceeded expectations, and morale soared. Pride became contagious. Employees were motivated not just by external recognition but by internal fulfillment. It wasn't just about getting the job done; it was about knowing they mattered in the bigger picture.

THE CHALLENGES AND TRIUMPHS OF LEADING WITH PRIDE

In a recent role as a vice president of retail, I encountered a team facing low morale and internal tensions. Despite the challenges, I saw it as an opportunity to rebuild and inspire pride. I made a promise: "Give me a chance, and I'll do everything I can to make a difference." This wasn't just about achieving results; it was about restoring pride in our work and rebuilding trust within the team.

Through open communication, recognition, and strategic changes, we began to see shifts. People started rediscovering their pride in their roles. Engagement and innovation flourished. Over three years, not a single original team member left, and we achieved record-breaking results. One powerful force rooted this transformation: pride.

THE TRANSFORMATIVE POWER OF PRIDE

Leadership grounded in pride is transformative. It's not a feel-good slogan; it's a strategic imperative. Leaders who inspire pride create environments where innovation, collaboration, and creativity thrive. It's about elevating not just the work but the people behind it.

Leadership grounded in pride is transformative. It's not a feel-good slogan; it's a strategic imperative.

When leaders cultivate pride in their teams, they set the stage for a workplace where individuals feel empowered to innovate and excel. They create cultures where success is measured in more than just outcomes, but in the growth, satisfaction, and resilience of every person involved.

YOUR LEADERSHIP LEGACY

The power of pride in leadership goes beyond daily achievements. It's about building a legacy of purpose and achievement. By nurturing pride, you elevate others, create a culture of respect and innovation, and inspire success that lasts far beyond your own contributions.

As you move forward in your leadership journey, I encourage you to step into your role as a pride-driven leader.

As you move forward in your leadership journey, I encourage you to step into your role as a pride-driven leader. Honor the human element of your team. Empower your colleagues, inspire growth, and ignite pride in every person you lead. This is the essence of **transformative leadership**, and it's time for you to step into it.

REFLECTION: TAPPING INTO THE POWER OF HUMAN PRIDE

Before we dive into the practical applications of this chapter, let's take a moment for reflection. Leadership rooted in pride starts with self-awareness. It's about recognizing your pride and how it impacts your career and the careers of those you lead. Pride is a force that transcends industries—it empowers, it uplifts, and it drives greatness.

Reflection Questions

1. **When was the last time you felt genuinely proud of your work**, and what was it about that experience that resonated so deeply with you? Was it the effort, the recognition, the collaboration, or the outcome? How can you recreate these moments for yourself and your team?

2. **How do you celebrate and nurture pride within your team?** Reflect on how you acknowledge contributions, growth, and effort. Are there ways you can intentionally create an environment where your team feels valued and connected to the work they do?

3. **What's one moment in your career when a leader made you feel seen and appreciated?** Think about how that moment influenced your confidence, motivation, and sense of belonging. How can you replicate that impact for others?

These questions will help guide your leadership journey. By understanding the importance of pride in leadership and embracing it as a powerful force, you will create an environment where excellence and growth are the natural outcomes.

Unleash the power of pride and transform your leadership. It's time to ignite change and inspire greatness within yourself and those around you.

IGNITE HUMAN PRIDE:
FIVE TRANSFORMATIVE LEADERSHIP PRINCIPLES

When I say, "Shine a light on excellence wherever you see it," I mean it with deep conviction. Many organizations far too often overlook the simple act of recognizing achievements, despite its proven ability to drive engagement and foster a sense of pride.

Principle One. Celebrate Achievements:
Elevating Recognition to Drive Engagement

In an era where employee retention remains a challenge, acknowledging individual and team accomplishments can be the catalyst for transforming the work environment.

> **Recognition, when done right, is not just a formality—it's a potent force that fuels pride and inspires a culture of excellence.**

Recognition, when done right, is not just a formality—it's a potent force that fuels pride and inspires a culture of excellence. By celebrating both the big wins and the smaller, everyday efforts, you not only boost morale but also deepen the commitment employees have toward their roles. Recognition validates their contributions, letting them know they are seen, heard, and appreciated. This simple act transforms ordinary moments into something extraordinary, igniting a collective energy that drives everyone forward.

Imagine a colleague's exceptional effort being highlighted on a company-wide message board or an innovative idea from your team getting public acknowledgment. These moments motivate, energize, and excite people about their work. It's not just about ticking off accomplishments—it's about inspiring pride in every member of your team.

Public recognition does more than highlight individual achievements; it reinforces a shared sense of purpose and collective success. It shows everyone that their individual efforts have a direct impact on the organization's overall mission, which creates a powerful sense of belonging and pride. When recognition is a natural part of the company culture, employees become eager to contribute more, collaborate better, and pioneer innovation.

Imagine a workplace where acknowledgment is not just given after an extensive project but woven into everyday interactions. The ripple effect of this culture is transformational. As pride spreads, so too does the enthusiasm to contribute, create, and excel—an energy that propels everyone toward higher performance.

Practical Strategies to Cultivate Recognition

▶ **Peer Recognition Initiatives:** Empower team members to recognize each other's contributions. Create spaces where employees can praise one another, such as a "Shout-Out" wall or a digital platform for posting appreciation notes. This simple practice strengthens bonds and ensures that pride is shared across the team.

▶ **Celebrate Growth:** Recognition isn't just about finished projects; it's about growth. Host quarterly events that spotlight personal milestones, such as certifications or new skills learned. When growth is celebrated, employees feel inspired to continuously develop, knowing the company values their progress.

▶ **Special Recognition Days:** Create themed events like "Innovation Day" or "Teamwork Tuesdays." These days offer the opportunity to celebrate creativity, collaboration, and success, bringing teams together to share and appreciate each other's achievements.

▶ **Town Hall Highlights:** In company-wide meetings, showcase individual and team accomplishments. This affirms each contribution, increases morale, and aligns employees with the company's mission, fostering a collective sense of pride in what they're achieving together.

▶ **Success Story Spotlights:** Use newsletters and internal communications to feature standout achievements. Sharing success stories boosts confidence and illustrates the power of collaboration, inspiring others to aim higher.

▶ **Monthly Awards Program:** Recognize exceptional efforts through awards like "Collaborator of the Month" or "Innovator of the Month." These accolades not only honor high performance but also inspire others, knowing their hard work will get noticed and celebrated.

Building a Culture of Acknowledgment

A culture of recognition is more than a workplace initiative—it's a commitment to building a thriving environment where pride is nurtured. When people feel truly valued, their motivation grows naturally. They feel connected to their work, to their colleagues, and to the mission of the company, creating an atmosphere of mutual respect, shared success, and collective ambition.

As pride deepens, so does the commitment to excellence.

Celebrating achievements has an immeasurable impact. Every moment of recognition is an investment in your team's future. As pride deepens, so does the commitment to excellence. This culture of acknowledgment fuels performance, collaboration, growth, and long-term success.

By fostering an environment where recognition is abundant, you lay the foundation for a culture of pride—one that drives engagement, innovation, and excellence across every level of the organization. This culture attracts and keeps top talent, encourages continuous growth, and inspires every team member to show up every day ready to give their best.

Start today—celebrate the contributions of your team and watch pride ignite new levels of collaboration and success. Lead with recognition and elevate your team toward greatness.

Principle Two. Empower Through Gratitude: Building Confidence and Enhancing Performance

A culture of **gratitude** has the power to transform a workplace into a vibrant, energized community where every person feels valued and motivated. When leaders consistently acknowledge their team's contributions, they create an environment where pride and purpose thrive, making gratitude not just a practice, but a driving force for engagement and success.

It's easy to underestimate the power of gratitude, yet its impact is profound and far-reaching. When people are appreciated for their contributions, they feel a stronger sense of belonging and commitment. This sense of appreciation doesn't just make people feel good—it empowers them. They take ownership of their work, invest more deeply in their roles, and inspire others to elevate their efforts. Gratitude isn't just recognition; it's a catalyst for connection, motivation, and shared achievement.

> **Gratitude isn't just recognition; it's a catalyst for connection, motivation, and shared achievement.**

Gratitude, when practiced consistently, unlocks an environment where innovation and continuous improvement become natural. Employees who feel valued are not just content with the status quo—they share ideas, tackle challenges, and propose creative solutions. As pride grows within the team, the enthusiasm and collaboration amplify, allowing everyone to thrive. It's this shared sense of purpose that propels the team to new heights of performance.

Reflecting on my experience as a vice president of stores, I discovered handwritten thank-you notes became one of the most effective ways to build a culture of gratitude. On the first Monday of each month, I made it a point to personally thank team members for their exceptional contributions. These small, heartfelt notes often found a permanent place on desks and bulletin boards as constant reminders their work was noticed and appreciated.

> **These small, heartfelt notes often found a permanent place on desks and bulletin boards as constant reminders their work was noticed and appreciated.**

This personal touch went far beyond any formal recognition. It created an environment where individuals felt a deeper connection to their work, knowing that their effort was not only acknowledged but celebrated. Pairing these notes with formal rewards created a balanced approach to recognition, one that had a tangible and lasting impact on engagement. This culture of gratitude became the foundation for a thriving workplace—one where pride, productivity, and shared success were the driving forces behind our achievements.

Blending Traditional and Modern Approaches to Recognition

Incorporating both traditional methods like handwritten notes and modern tools like digital recognition platforms or public shout-outs provides a well-rounded approach to fostering pride and engagement. Imagine a workplace where tangible rewards are complemented by sincere expressions of gratitude—this layered recognition system strengthens connections within the team, ensuring every contribution, no matter how big or small, is valued.

Practical Strategies to Strengthen Recognition

- ▷ **Recognition Circles:** Regular meetings where team members share acknowledgments and celebrate each other's achievements help reinforce a culture of appreciation. Rotating leadership within these sessions fosters inclusivity and offers fresh perspectives, creating unity and mutual respect.
- ▷ **Showcase Success Stories:** Dedicate time during meetings and in newsletters to highlight achievements. These success stories showcase the impact of individual and team efforts and inspire others to reflect on their contributions, fostering an atmosphere of pride.
- ▷ **Empowerment Projects:** Provide opportunities for employees to lead initiatives or propose solutions, recognizing their

contributions with public acknowledgment or professional development incentives. This empowers employees to take ownership of their work and feel proud of their impact.

▶ **Gratitude Boards:** Create a physical or digital space where team members can leave notes of appreciation for one another. This simple, effective tool fosters a positive atmosphere and strengthens relationships within the team, building a foundation of mutual respect and collaboration.

▶ **Peer-Led Workshops:** Encourage colleagues to share their expertise and insights through workshops. This highlights individual strengths while promoting shared learning and collaboration, further enriching the workplace culture and building a supportive environment.

The Impact of Gratitude

By making gratitude an integral part of your leadership, you inspire pride, enhance performance, and create a positive cycle of motivation and engagement. Gratitude shows that every effort matters, cultivating a shared sense of purpose and fostering an environment where everyone feels seen and valued.

> **Start small. Write a note, send a message, or publicly acknowledge someone's contributions.**

Start small. Write a note, send a message, or publicly acknowledge someone's contributions. Observe how these simple acts of appreciation generate positive energy throughout your workplace. As you do, you'll create a culture of collaboration, growth, and success—a place where pride and engagement flourish and where every team member feels empowered to bring their best self to work every day.

Together, let's champion recognition and create a thriving, inclusive environment that celebrates and uplifts every contributor. Start today—let gratitude become your leadership superpower!

Principle Three. Build Trust and Elevate Performance through the Power of Confident Teams

Trust is the cornerstone of any thriving workplace. It's the invisible thread that binds people together, creating a foundation where individuals feel empowered to take initiative, share ideas, and collaborate freely. Leaders who prioritize building trust within their teams unlock exceptional potential, drive innovation, and foster resilience, creating an environment where everyone feels valued and motivated to contribute their best.

In my leadership journey, I've seen firsthand how trust transforms teams. Trust doesn't just fuel collaboration; it inspires confidence and empowerment. When teams know they can rely on one another, they feel more secure in taking risks, tackle challenges head-on, and embrace creativity without fear of judgment. This leads to a stronger sense of ownership, ensuring each team member is invested in their work and its success. When trust is present, a team operates not just as individuals but as a cohesive unit, working toward a shared vision with purpose.

We build trust through consistent actions, open communication, and a commitment to recognizing the contributions of each individual.

However, we must intentionally cultivate trust; it doesn't simply appear. Leaders must actively create environments where team members feel respected, supported, and confident in their abilities. We build trust through consistent actions, open communication, and a commitment to recognizing the contributions of each individual. When leaders show trust in their teams, they affirm that every member's contribution matters, reinforcing the collective belief that everyone plays a pivotal role in the team's success.

One way to build trust is by fostering **collaboration** across departments. When you encourage cross-functional teams, you create an atmosphere where different perspectives can shine, driving fresh ideas and innovative solutions. By demonstrating you trust your team to tackle these initiatives, you also empower them to step outside their comfort zones, boosting their confidence and engagement.

> **When employees have the freedom to make decisions and experiment within their roles, they build a stronger connection to their work.**

Providing **autonomy** is another crucial aspect of building trust. When employees have the freedom to make decisions and experiment within their roles, they build a stronger connection to their work. Autonomy enables team members to feel more invested in their contributions and confident in their problem-solving abilities. Pairing autonomy with constructive feedback ensures they feel supported in their growth, creating a culture of continuous improvement where mistakes are valuable learning opportunities.

Practical Strategies to Build and Sustain Trust

Here are several actionable steps you can take to build and sustain trust within your team:

- ▶ **Create Cross-Functional Teams:** Bring together team members from various departments to work on challenges or innovative projects. This fosters creativity, demonstrates your belief in their capabilities, and strengthens the interconnectedness of the organization.

- ► **Support Innovation Through Resources:** Encourage employees to pitch new ideas and offer resources to help test and implement them. This shows your trust in their creativity, motivating them to think boldly and drive growth both personally and within the organization.

- ► **Encourage Peer-Led Learning:** Give team members the opportunity to lead workshops or share their expertise with the group. This recognition reinforces collaboration and helps foster a culture of mutual respect and continuous learning.

- ► **Turn Mistakes into Lessons:** Transform setbacks into valuable opportunities for growth. Discuss what went wrong, what lessons can be learned, and how the team can collaborate to find solutions. This encourages resilience, reduces fear of failure, and keeps the innovation flowing.

- ► **Involve New Voices in Decision-Making:** Involve team members from all levels in decision-making processes. Fresh perspectives lead to innovative solutions, and regularly including new voices shows everyone's input is valued.

The Ripple Effect of Trust

When you implement these strategies, you create an environment where trust fuels not only collaboration and innovation but also pride in the work being done. When team members feel trusted and valued, they are more likely to work harder and contribute new ideas.

This shared trust results in a cohesive team where everyone is motivated to push their limits and achieve extraordinary outcomes. When leaders build and maintain trust, they create lasting change, fostering an environment that thrives on collaboration, creativity, and mutual respect.

Trust is the bridge connecting individual potential to organizational success. It empowers teams to take ownership of their work and perform at their highest level, enabling long-term success. By committing to a leadership approach rooted in trust, you're not only driving results—you're creating a team dynamic where everyone feels connected, valued, and ready to contribute their best.

> **Trust is the bridge connecting individual potential to organizational success.**

Takeaway: Lead with Trust

Start building trust within your team by fostering open communication, giving employees the freedom to innovate, and actively recognizing their contributions. Watch as trust strengthens your team's resilience, drives their engagement, and unlocks a culture of creativity and success. When you lead with trust, you not only elevate individual performance—you transform the entire organization. Commit to trust and watch your team thrive.

Principle Four. Communicate with Impact by Turning Words into Leadership Action

Here's the bold truth: without exceptional communication, you can't inspire pride in your team. **Communication** isn't just a skill—it's the foundation of effective leadership. Your ability to articulate a clear vision and connect with others is essential for motivating, guiding, and inspiring action. At its heart, great communication turns your vision into a shared purpose that energizes and unites your team.

When expectations are unclear, people feel lost, disconnected, and unsure of their roles. This confusion undermines motivation and engagement. Exceptional communication eliminates these barriers, replacing uncertainty with shared purpose and alignment. By explaining the "what" and "why" behind goals, leaders empower their teams to contribute to collective success.

Communication is more than words—it's about connection. It's the bridge that helps your team navigate challenges, seize opportunities, and grow together. Leaders who communicate with clarity and authenticity foster environments where collaboration thrives, creativity flows, and team members feel confident in their contributions.

To lead effectively, you must master both delivering messages and active listening. Communication goes beyond sharing information—it's about building trust, understanding, and collaborating. When people feel heard, they're more likely to invest their energy and talents in achieving shared goals. Engaging dialogue creates a climate of innovation and teamwork, strengthening bonds and driving results.

Elevating Your Communication

Are you ready to transform how you connect with your team? Enhancing communication requires practice, commitment, and adaptability. It's not about perfection—it's about progress and the positive ripple effects your efforts create. Invest in improving your skills through workshops, books, and peer discussions. Seek feedback to refine your approach and create opportunities for open conversations with your team.

Leaders who communicate with purpose foster unity, inspire pride, and drive results.

> **Leaders who communicate with purpose foster unity, inspire pride, and drive results.**

Exceptional communication begins with intentionality. Each conversation, presentation, or message is a chance to build trust, clarify goals, and strengthen your team's shared vision. Leaders who communicate with purpose foster unity, inspire pride, and drive results.

Best Practices for Transformative Communication

- ▶ **Adopt a Growth Mindset:** Believing in the power of improvement is key to impactful communication. Use feedback to grow, demonstrating resilience and adaptability. When your team sees your commitment to learning, they're inspired to do the same, reinforcing a culture of continuous improvement and collaboration.

- ▶ **Provide Multiple Feedback Channels:** Everyone has unique preferences for giving and receiving feedback. Offer options like one-on-ones, anonymous surveys, and open forums to foster trust and belonging. When people see their feedback leading to real changes, engagement and morale rise, strengthening their connection to the team's mission.

- ▶ **Train Your Team in Feedback Skills:** Equip team members with the tools to offer and receive constructive feedback effectively. To establish open dialogue, model empathy, patience, and active listening. Eventually, this creates a workplace where people respect each other and solve problems before they get worse.

- ▶ **Commit to Regular Check-Ins:** Frequent touchpoints strengthen relationships, clarify objectives, and address concerns. Use these moments to celebrate achievements, solve problems, and ensure alignment. Regular check-ins foster pride, build trust, and create a sense of shared purpose.

- ▶ **Focus on Solutions:** Encourage a "How can we solve this?" mindset during discussions. This approach motivates team members to contribute ideas and take ownership of outcomes, fostering resilience, collaboration, and confidence.

The Transformational Power of Communication

Prioritizing clear, impactful communication amplifies leadership effectiveness and creates a workplace where everyone feels valued and empowered. Each meaningful interaction builds accountability, deepens connections, and reinforces shared success.

Exceptional communication isn't just about words—it's about building trust, inspiring action, and fostering a culture of pride and collaboration.

Exceptional communication isn't just about words— it's about building trust, inspiring action, and fostering a culture of pride and collaboration.

Leaders who master this skill create environments where vision becomes action, challenges turn into opportunities, and every team member feels integral to the mission.

By embracing these practices, you establish a legacy of inclusive, connected leadership. Every effort to improve communication elevates your influence while unlocking the potential and pride of those around you. Together, you can transform your workplace into a hub of collaboration, inspiration, and excellence.

Now is the time to lead with clarity, encourage open dialogue, and ignite your team's potential. Watch as your commitment inspires extraordinary results and builds a future defined by shared success and pride. Through the power of communication, you'll cultivate a workplace where every voice matters, every challenge sparks innovation, and every individual thrives as part of a unified team.

Principle Five. Lead with Joy: Inspiring Authenticity and Connection

We've discussed how identifying personal sources of joy helps define your nonnegotiables. Now, let's explore an even more impactful aspect: sparking that joy in those you lead. This is the essence of transformative leadership and a hallmark of human pride. By integrating gratitude, celebration, and moments of levity into your workplace, you can elevate morale, deepen connections, and inspire a thriving, motivated team. **Cultivating joy is one of the most human and powerful acts a leader can perform.**

Cultivating joy is one of the most human and powerful acts a leader can perform.

Authentic leadership starts with aligning actions to core values, fostering transparency, and building trust. Tackling challenges with openness and humor while embracing genuine moments of laughter creates a space where creativity thrives and belonging grows. Recognizing individual contributions doesn't just ignite pride—it strengthens bonds and propels collective achievement.

Being an authentic leader means embracing both strengths and vulnerabilities. Transparency and integrity build trust, encouraging full engagement from your team. Authenticity isn't about sacrificing professionalism; it's about leading with empathy, listening actively, and genuinely caring for your team's well-being. This approach empowers individuals to express themselves confidently, enhancing collaboration, and fostering a culture that celebrates diversity of thought and experience.

Consistency in aligning decisions with core values is key. Holding yourself accountable reinforces trust and bolsters your credibility. Sharing personal stories or lessons learned deepens team connections and showcases your humanity without undermining authority. This openness encourages others to embrace their true selves, creating a dynamic and motivated environment.

Reflecting on my journey, I once believed projecting seriousness was essential for authority. Fear of seeming too casual held me back from showing my authentic self. Embracing the principles of "Live, Laugh, and Learn" revealed the power of joy and openness. These principles elevated morale, strengthened bonds, and fostered a positive atmosphere that empowered my team to excel.

One vital lesson: transparency and continuous learning don't weaken authority—they strengthen it. Leaders don't need all the answers. By modeling adaptability and sharing your growth journey, you inspire your team to view challenges as opportunities. When people see their development prioritized—through workshops, mentorship, or skill-building—they feel valued, reinforcing pride and engagement.

> **One vital lesson: transparency and continuous learning don't weaken authority— they strengthen it.**

Strategies to Infuse Joy and Authenticity into Leadership

> ▶ **Host Joyful Leadership Workshops:** Design interactive sessions focused on celebrating wins, tackling challenges creatively, and sharing personal anecdotes of joy. Use

role-playing, storytelling, and collaborative games to build camaraderie and demonstrate the link between joy and productivity.

▶ **Designate Wednesdays as Wellness Wednesdays:** Dedicate each to activities such as meditation, yoga, painting, or baking. Shared experiences reduce stress, strengthen connections, and show your commitment to team well-being, fostering pride and a positive environment.

▶ **Launch a Mentorship Program:** Pair experienced team members with newer colleagues to encourage knowledge sharing and growth. This initiative empowers mentees to explore their strengths and gives mentors fulfillment in guiding others, creating a culture of continuous learning and mutual pride.

The Transformational Impact of Joyful Leadership

By embedding joy and authenticity into your leadership style, you create an extraordinary workplace where everyone feels valued and inspired. Together, you and your team cultivate a culture of pride, innovation, and shared success, setting the foundation for a vibrant and inclusive future.

Exceptional leadership begins with a commitment to these principles. It's about crafting a workplace that's not just productive but joyful, growth-oriented, and inclusive. As a catalyst for this change, you'll see your team thrive, united by pride and shared purpose. The impact of leading with joy resonates not only in results but also in the lives of those you inspire.

> **The impact of leading with joy resonates not only in results but also in the lives of those you inspire.**

ESSENTIAL TAKEAWAYS FOR DRIVING ENGAGEMENT AND EXCELLENCE

Human pride isn't just a by-product of success—it's the fuel that drives you to engage, persevere, and achieve.

Human Pride as Your Cornerstone for Engagement and Achievement

When you take pride in your work, you naturally strive for excellence, take accountability, and contribute with genuine passion. This pride ignites a commitment to giving your best every day, elevating your work and inspiring those around you.

By celebrating accomplishments—whether your own or others'— you reinforce pride, cultivating a culture where striving for greatness becomes second nature. Leaders who nurture and recognize pride create spaces where you can perform at your highest level, enabling you to leave a legacy of growth and success.

Building Trust to Unlock Your Excellence

Trust is the foundation of everything you achieve. It empowers you to take initiative, share bold ideas, and face challenges without fear of judgment. When leaders trust their teams, they create an environment where creativity flourishes and collaboration becomes effortless.

Imagine working in a space where your contributions are valued, your efforts are acknowledged, and your voice is heard. Trust fosters resilience and strengthens relationships, helping you tackle obstacles and pursue ambitious goals with confidence. By prioritizing trust, you and your team can unlock new levels of excellence and success.

The Impact of Clear and Empathetic Communication

Clear and empathetic communication is the bridge that connects your goals to action. It aligns teams, builds understanding, and ensures that everyone knows their role in achieving success. When you receive clear direction and honest feedback, you feel confident, focused, and empowered to do your best work.

Leaders who communicate transparently and with empathy don't just convey information—they foster a shared purpose. When you understand how your contributions fit into the bigger picture, you feel a deeper sense of ownership and pride in what you do. Empathy ensures that communication is inclusive and human-centered, making you feel valued and heard.

Infusing Joy and Authenticity into Your Leadership

Joy and authenticity aren't optional—they are transformative forces. When leaders embrace their true selves and live their values, they foster trust, deepen connections, and create a culture where you bring your complete self to work.

Think about the power of a genuine "thank you," a moment of levity, or the celebration of your unique strengths. These moments infuse energy into your day, sparking creativity and building a workplace where you feel both valued and inspired. Authenticity inspires you to show up fully, contributing to shared goals while feeling seen and appreciated for who you are.

Recognition as a Driver of Your Growth and Innovation

Recognition is a powerful motivator—it reinforces your efforts, strengthens your confidence, and inspires you to reach higher.

When your contributions are acknowledged, whether big or small, it validates your role and motivates you to continue innovating.

Imagine the momentum that builds when you're consistently recognized for your hard work. From a simple thank-you to public accolades, meaningful recognition fosters a culture of appreciation and pride. It encourages you to explore your potential and collaborate more creatively, knowing your efforts are making a difference.

Final Reflection: Moving Forward with Human Pride

The transformative power of human pride lies in its ability to elevate you, foster collaboration, and create a culture of excellence. By embracing these principles—cultivating pride, building trust, communicating with empathy, leading authentically, and celebrating recognition—you can thrive in any environment and inspire those around you to do the same.

The transformative power of human pride lies in its ability to elevate you, foster collaboration, and create a culture of excellence.

This isn't just about achieving success—it's about celebrating your humanity. When you prioritize these values, you unlock your full potential and create a legacy of shared purpose, innovation, and growth. You have the power to lead with pride, connect with others, and achieve greatness. The world is waiting for your light—step forward and let it shine.

YOUR NEXT STEPS: ELEVATING PRIDE WITHIN YOUR TEAM

Human pride is a transformative force in leadership, driving engagement, performance, and innovation. To lead effectively, you must inspire pride within your team by fostering connection, trust, and recognition. These actions will help you integrate the principles of human pride into your leadership approach, creating an environment where everyone thrives.

1. Celebrate Achievements Regularly

Recognition is a cornerstone of pride and motivation.

- ▶ Identify and acknowledge individual and team accomplishments, no matter the size.
- ▶ Celebrate growth, innovation, and milestones to highlight the value of every contribution.

Action Step: This week, identify one team member or group to spotlight for their efforts. Share specific details about their impact in a meeting or through a written message.

2. Build Trust Through Empowerment

Trust unlocks creativity, accountability, and collaboration.

- ▶ Provide team members with autonomy and opportunities to lead initiatives.
- ▶ Encourage risk-taking and support a "fail forward" mindset to foster resilience and innovation.

Action Step: Identify one task to delegate this month, ensuring the person has the resources and confidence to succeed. Follow up with feedback to reinforce trust and growth.

3. Communicate with Clarity and Empathy

Effective communication strengthens alignment and engagement.

- ▶ Articulate your vision and expectations while inviting open dialogue.
- ▶ Practice active listening to ensure everyone feels heard and valued.

Action Step: Schedule one-on-one check-ins with your team members to discuss their goals, challenges, and contributions. Use these conversations to align expectations and provide support.

4. Infuse Joy into Your Leadership

Joy fosters connection, innovation, and a sense of belonging.

- ▶ Create moments of lightheartedness and gratitude in your workplace.
- ▶ Celebrate shared successes and personal milestones to enhance camaraderie.

Action Step: Host a team activity, such as a casual lunch or a creative workshop, to encourage bonding and shared joy. Use this time to highlight recent successes and express gratitude.

5. Foster a Culture of Continuous Recognition

Acknowledgment inspires pride and drives sustained excellence.

- ▶ Develop systems for ongoing recognition, such as peer shout-outs or monthly awards.
- ▶ Encourage team members to celebrate each other's contributions regularly.

Action Step: Launch a peer recognition program where colleagues can nominate each other for their achievements. Share these nominations during team meetings to increase their impact.

Your Leadership Legacy

Leadership grounded in human pride transforms not just individual performance but also team dynamics and organizational culture. By celebrating achievements, building trust, fostering joy, and prioritizing clear communication, you create a workplace where everyone feels valued and empowered.

> **By celebrating achievements, building trust, fostering joy, and prioritizing clear communication, you create a workplace where everyone feels valued and empowered.**

Take pride in the positive changes you inspire and in your commitment to cultivating a culture of excellence. Every step you take toward prioritizing human pride strengthens your team and your leadership impact, building a future defined by shared success and authentic connection.

Leadership in this context is about more than achieving operational goals— it's about crafting a legacy of inclusion, empowerment, and pride.

CHAPTER 6

LEADING FROM THE HEART

Building Inclusivity and Authenticity

We lead people—complex, dynamic, messy, and multifaceted beings with unique experiences, perspectives, and aspirations. Our success as leaders depends on our ability to compassionately, flexibly, and intentionally address these complexities. Cultivating pride within a team is both an art and a responsibility, demanding that we navigate diverse dynamics with unwavering care and clarity.

As we've explored throughout this book, pride is a driving force for both personal fulfillment and professional excellence. It is not just an emotional state—it is a catalyst that propels individuals to recognize their value, pursue greater goals, and contribute

Fostering an environment where pride flourishes is not just a noble ambition; it is essential for unlocking the collective potential of any team.

meaningfully. Whether in retail settings, navigating modern workplace challenges, or inspiring diverse groups, the impact of pride is undeniable. Fostering an environment where pride flourishes is not just a noble ambition; it is essential for unlocking the collective potential of any team.

Authenticity and **inclusivity**, the foundational principles of transformative leadership, lie at the heart of this mission.

WHY AUTHENTICITY AND INCLUSIVITY MATTER

Authenticity and inclusivity define the essence of a thriving workplace. When leaders model authenticity, they invite their teams to show up as their true selves, cultivating an atmosphere of psychological safety, trust, and mutual respect. Inclusivity builds upon this foundation, ensuring every individual feels valued for their unique perspectives and contributions. Together, these principles create a space where collaboration and innovation flourish, amplifying the collective strength of the group.

> **Authenticity and inclusivity define the essence of a thriving workplace.**

When people feel seen, heard, and valued, their engagement deepens. They share ideas with enthusiasm, encourage one another, and strive toward shared goals with passion. This climate of inclusivity and authenticity enables teams to adapt and thrive in today's fast-evolving professional landscape.

THE LEADERSHIP CHALLENGE: STARTING THE JOURNEY

Creating this kind of workplace culture may seem like a lofty goal, but the journey begins with asking the right questions: "Where are the barriers to inclusivity in my organization?" and "What steps can I take to foster authenticity and mutual respect?" These reflections serve as the compass for leaders making meaningful changes.

The first challenge lies in identifying and addressing systemic obstacles—hierarchical structures, lack of transparency, or siloed communication—that stifle collaboration and innovation. Rapid workplace evolution has heightened these issues, making proactive and thoughtful strategies more essential than ever.

Leaders must serve as role models, embodying the behaviors they wish to inspire. This includes embracing diverse perspectives, prioritizing transparency, and showing genuine gratitude for contributions. Leadership is not about directing from above; it's about uplifting others, celebrating their individuality, and fostering a culture of shared accountability.

LEADERSHIP AS A CATALYST FOR COLLECTIVE GROWTH

Authentic leadership is about more than achieving goals; it's about empowering people to achieve their fullest potential. By prioritizing the growth of others, leaders create environments where individuals feel motivated to excel, strengthening the overall team. Framing success as a collective endeavor shifts the energy from competition to collaboration, leading to extraordinary results.

> **Authentic leadership is about more than achieving goals; it's about empowering people to achieve their fullest potential.**

Leadership is not static—it evolves with time, challenges, and the needs of the team. Reflection and adaptability are key to maintaining relevance and effectiveness. A leadership approach that resonates in one situation may require refinement in another. This iterative process, grounded in pride and guided by empathy, ensures leaders can meet the unique needs of their teams while remaining true to their core values.

ADAPTING FOR IMPACT

Effective leadership defies rigid categorization. It demands a nuanced understanding of the people you lead, the challenges they face, and the context in which they operate. Leaders who listen deeply, observe thoughtfully, and respond with intention foster a culture of trust and mutual respect.

Leaders who listen deeply, observe thoughtfully, and respond with intention foster a culture of trust and mutual respect.

This adaptability may manifest in varied ways—offering clear guidance during times of crisis, engaging in open collaboration to spark innovation, or providing reassurance during moments of uncertainty. These tailored approaches demonstrate a leader's commitment to their team's success, inspiring confidence and loyalty.

By embracing adaptability, leaders build relationships rooted in empathy and understanding, cultivating an environment where people feel empowered to contribute their best selves.

A FRAMEWORK FOR INCLUSIVE LEADERSHIP

In the next section, you will explore a practical framework for building inclusive, high-performing teams that are poised for sustained success. These principles challenge conventional leadership models, emphasizing the value of diverse perspectives and experiences in achieving exceptional outcomes.

By focusing on inclusivity as a cornerstone of leadership, you will learn to create environments where individuals feel empowered to showcase their unique strengths. In such spaces, engagement deepens, trust strengthens, and collaboration flourishes. Barriers dissolve as respect and shared purpose drive the team forward, transforming challenges into opportunities for innovation and collective achievement.

Prepare to discover how inclusivity can redefine success for your team and your organization, turning aspirations into tangible, transformative outcomes.

REFLECTION: CONNECTING WITH THE HEART OF LEADERSHIP

Before diving into the framework, let's pause for a moment of reflection. Reflection allows us to connect deeply with our intentions and experiences, uncovering insights that elevate our leadership approach. It's a moment to step back, consider the impact we want to create, and recognize the opportunities we have to lead with empathy, courage, and clarity.

Leadership rooted in authenticity and inclusivity begins with self-awareness. By exploring our values, assumptions, and biases, we pave the way for growth—both in ourselves and in those we lead. Reflection is not just about finding answers but about asking the right questions to guide us toward meaningful action.

Take this time to reflect on your journey as a leader. These questions inspire deeper connection and understanding, helping you unlock the potential for transformative leadership within yourself and your team.

Reflection Questions

1. **How do you show authenticity in your leadership?** Reflect on moments when you've shown vulnerability, shared your true self, or invited others to do the same. How have these actions shaped trust and collaboration within your team?

2. **What steps have you taken to create an inclusive environment where diverse perspectives are valued?** Consider whether your leadership fosters openness and belonging. Are there areas where voices go unheard or where opportunities for growth and connection might be expanded?

3. **When was the last time you truly listened to understand rather than to respond?** Think about how active listening has deepened your relationships and enhanced your team's creativity and cohesion. How can you cultivate more moments of connection and understanding?

Let these questions guide you as you move forward. Authenticity and inclusivity are not static achievements; they are ongoing commitments that evolve with intention and care. By engaging in this reflection, you honor the heart of leadership and prepare yourself to lead with greater clarity, compassion, and impact.

FIVE STRATEGIES TO EMPOWER THROUGH INCLUSIVITY

Here are five practical strategies that you, as a leader, can use to create a more inclusive and empowering workplace.

Strategy One. Empowering Through Inclusivity:
Building a Culture of Belonging

Amber Cabral's podcast, *Guilty Privilege*, provides a profound lens through which we can examine privilege and bias in our workplaces and communities. Her impactful insights have been instrumental in shaping my leadership philosophy, particularly when it comes to navigating issues of race, allyship, and systemic inequality. In 2020, I had the privilege of collaborating with Amber during pivotal conversations surrounding these topics. Her guidance helped my organization approach sensitive discussions with courage, empathy, and clarity.

Through her work, Amber emphasizes how privilege manifests in both subtle and overt ways—often unnoticed by those who benefit from it. This awareness can only begin with honest self-reflection and the willingness to confront uncomfortable truths. Resistance, particularly from those hesitant to examine their own privileges, is natural. Yet meaningful and lasting change requires leadership that is steadfast in its commitment to **equity**.

True equity begins with the acknowledgment of privilege and unconscious bias in all of us. It is through this awareness that change begins. Implementing bias-awareness training and sparking important conversations around privilege can uncover hidden prejudices. These actions pave the way for equitable hiring, career development, and promotion practices, ensuring that everyone in the workplace feels valued and empowered to contribute.

True equity begins with the acknowledgment of privilege and unconscious bias in all of us.

This work is neither swift nor simple, but it is essential. Building an equitable workplace is not merely a business priority—it is a moral commitment. It is about creating an environment where people genuinely thrive. Leaders who prioritize open dialogue, embrace ongoing learning, and consistently support their teams lay the foundation for sustainable success.

Leadership in this context is about more than achieving operational goals—it's about crafting a legacy of inclusion, empowerment, and pride.

Leadership in this context is about more than achieving operational goals—it's about crafting a legacy of inclusion, empowerment, and pride. By recognizing bias and taking decisive action, leaders can unlock the potential that exists within each person, driving collective achievement and producing innovative results.

Let's embark on this journey together. By addressing privilege and bias with intentionality, we can create transformative change. Consider the following actionable initiatives to bring this vision to life:

▶ **Structured Mentorship Programs:** Connect underrepresented employees with senior leaders. This helps foster relationships that provide growth opportunities. Training mentors in cultural competency and allyship ensures these programs deliver fair outcomes while preparing diverse talent for leadership roles.

▶ **Inclusive Job Descriptions:** Reframe hiring practices to prioritize competencies, adaptability, and potential over rigid qualifications like "five-plus years of experience." This broadens the talent pool, enriching workplace diversity and unlocking innovation.

- **Diverse Interview Panels:** Assemble interview panels that represent a variety of backgrounds. Provide unconscious bias training to ensure balanced evaluations and inclusivity from the very start of the hiring process.
- **Transparent Career Pathways:** Offer clear promotion criteria and structured mentorship. Workshops and a transparent promotion system allow employees to see the road to advancement and know that progress is based on merit, building trust and inspiring commitment.
- **Senior Leadership Commitment:** Inclusion starts at the top. Leaders and boards should set clear, measurable equity goals, share progress transparently, and align their actions with organizational values. By holding themselves accountable, they ensure inclusion is not just a passing initiative but a central and enduring priority.

Addressing privilege and bias is not a onetime effort but a collective, ongoing commitment. These strategies represent a promise to build workplaces where diversity is not only celebrated but actively encouraged. Everyone deserves the opportunity to succeed, and by fostering equity, we create cultures where innovation can thrive and extraordinary achievements become possible.

> **By challenging assumptions, educating ourselves, and fostering inclusivity, we unlock the transformative power of equity.**

By challenging assumptions, educating ourselves, and fostering inclusivity, we unlock the transformative power of equity. Together, we can create work environments where potential flourishes, innovation thrives, and remarkable achievements become reality.

Strategy Two. Defining Progress:
Measuring Inclusion to Drive Meaningful Change

The timeless adage "If you don't measure it, you can't manage it" has never been more pertinent, especially for inclusion. Establishing clear, actionable **metrics** for inclusion is fundamental to creating workplaces where pride and potential flourish. Traditionally, inclusion efforts have focused on race and ethnicity, but true inclusivity demands a more holistic approach. It must embrace sexual identity, income level, first-generation status, cultural background, gender expression, and other factors that influence workplace dynamics. By defining and tracking measurable inclusion goals, organizations can go beyond surface-level efforts, identify gaps, and drive transformative progress.

Metrics are powerful tools. They uncover hidden barriers, inequities, and opportunities for growth. For instance, data on workplace demographics, leadership diversity, and training participation provide actionable insights that shape impactful strategies. A data-driven approach aligns inclusion efforts with the workforce's specific needs, enabling leaders to take targeted actions for meaningful change.

At its core, pride and potential cannot thrive without understanding and measuring them.

At its core, pride and potential cannot thrive without understanding and measuring them. Without the right metrics, we cannot identify where we need improvement or where we are making progress.

Start by defining what inclusion means for your organization. This is not a one-size-fits-all approach—tailor the goals to fit your culture, values, and objectives. Understand that inclusion may manifest differently across departments, roles, and teams. For example, inclusion in leadership may require one set of metrics, while inclusion in entry-level positions may need another. Track trends, evaluate outcomes, and measure progress in areas such as leadership representation, career advancement, and employee engagement by using metrics. Regular reviews are not just administrative—they are opportunities for accountability, learning, and continuous growth.

Measuring success should inform training and development programs that close gaps and empower employees. Align these initiatives with measurable goals to enhance engagement and productivity. When employees see tangible evidence that inclusion efforts lead to their personal and professional growth, they feel more valued and connected. This strengthens pride in their roles and contributions.

Metrics tied to clear, actionable goals build a strong sense of ownership and commitment among employees. When we celebrate incremental progress, it creates a sense of unity and pride across the organization. This environment motivates everyone to contribute their best work, thus increasing collaboration and innovation.

Regularly reviewing metrics gives organizations clarity on resource allocation, policy adaptations, and initiative effectiveness.

A data-driven approach to decision-making also ensures fairness and transparency. Regularly reviewing metrics gives organizations clarity on resource allocation, policy adaptations, and initiative effectiveness. This transparency transforms inclusion from a lofty idea into a measurable, actionable force for progress.

Measuring inclusion isn't about the numbers—it's about creating a culture where every individual feels valued, capable, and empowered to contribute their best.

Actionable Steps for Measuring Inclusivity

- ▶ **Recruitment and Hiring Sources:** Analyze the sources of your candidates—whether that's job boards, referrals, or partnerships—and track diversity at every stage of hiring. By identifying potential barriers or biases, you can broaden access for underrepresented groups, ensuring more equitable opportunities.

- ▶ **Promotion and Career Advancement:** Examine promotion rates across various demographic groups to identify gaps in leadership opportunities. Addressing these disparities shows a commitment to equity and helps build trust and engagement within the organization.

- ▶ **Workplace Engagement and Satisfaction:** Conduct regular surveys to gauge employee perceptions of inclusion, leadership, and workplace satisfaction. Insights from a variety of voices will guide improvements, strengthening a culture of belonging and mutual respect.

- ▶ **Retention Rates:** Track turnover trends and identify patterns that highlight systemic challenges. If high turnover exists among specific groups, this should be a red flag. Analyzing retention rates ensures employees feel supported and motivated to remain with the organization.

- ▶ **Accountability and Transparency:** Review inclusion metrics regularly and set benchmarks to track progress. Make the findings public and share them with stakeholders to foster collective responsibility and demonstrate a genuine commitment to action.

Transforming Culture Through Measurement

Embrace inclusion as a foundational element of organizational culture because it fuels collaboration, innovation, and success. Measuring inclusion is not just about tracking numbers—it's about creating a culture where pride is fostered, where every voice is heard, and where everyone contributes to a shared vision.

By measuring, addressing, and celebrating inclusion, organizations can create environments where human pride thrives, resulting in exceptional outcomes and collective success. This

By measuring, addressing, and celebrating inclusion, organizations can create environments where human pride thrives, resulting in exceptional outcomes and collective success.

measurement-driven approach ensures that inclusion isn't just a lofty ideal but a dynamic, actionable mission that shapes a thriving, empowered workplace.

Strategy Three. Nurturing Potential: The Critical Role of Professional Development

Accessible and impactful **professional development** is a catalyst for pride and engagement in an organization. Prioritizing employee growth signals that their abilities are valued and their potential is recognized. Leaders who champion development opportunities cultivate a culture rooted in inclusivity, innovation, and shared success, benefiting both individuals and the organization.

Too often, organizations focus only on developing current leadership while neglecting the growth of emerging talent. Professional development and improving your skills don't mean others' skills decrease. A balanced approach, one that emphasizes both leadership training and broader initiatives, nurtures adaptability, collaboration, and continuous improvement at all levels of the workforce.

Imagine a workplace where growth isn't just an aspiration but a reality woven into the fabric of everyday work life.

Imagine a workplace where growth isn't just an aspiration but a reality woven into the fabric of everyday work life. Leaders who evolve alongside their teams create a resilient, skilled workforce ready to meet challenges head-on and seize new opportunities. These environments amplify individual pride and unlock collective potential, laying the groundwork for sustained excellence.

Strategies for Meaningful Development Opportunities

Comprehensive Leadership Programs

Design structured programs that combine mentorship, workshops, and hands-on projects. Pair emerging leaders with seasoned mentors to share knowledge and foster growth. Focus on building core competencies like emotional intelligence, decision-making, and inclusive leadership to prepare leaders for complex challenges.

These programs form a robust leadership pipeline, ensuring the seamless transfer of knowledge and capabilities. Employees trust the process, feeling valued by the organization's investment in their success. Adaptive leadership training reinforces collaboration and future-focused thinking, ensuring leadership evolves with the demands of the workforce.

Personalized Growth Plans

Collaborate with employees to create individualized development roadmaps tailored to their career aspirations. By identifying key skills, pursuing targeted learning opportunities, and setting clear milestones, employees take ownership of their growth, which boosts pride and engagement.

Personalized plans also show the company's commitment to supporting diverse ambitions. Aligning individual goals with organizational objectives deepens employees' sense of loyalty and motivation.

Cross-Departmental Learning

Encourage job rotations and cross-functional projects to broaden employees' skills and perspectives. Exposure to different departments enhances innovation, strengthens teamwork, and fosters a deeper understanding of the organization's operations.

These experiences break down silos, promote collaboration, and create a shared purpose. Learning new processes and approaches helps employees feel connected to the company's broader mission, boosting pride and mutual respect across departments.

Technology-Driven Training

Use online platforms to continuously improve your leadership, technical skills, and emotional intelligence. Offer access to webinars, e-learning modules, and industry conferences to promote independent learning and keep teams informed of the latest trends.

Offering flexible, accessible training ensures that all roles, regardless of time or location, can benefit. Equipped with current knowledge, employees gain confidence and accountability, inspiring pride in their continued growth.

Feedback and Reflection

Establish a culture where feedback flows openly and reflection is integral to learning. Regularly solicit employee input on training programs to ensure they align with evolving needs and professional aspirations. Celebrate milestones and progress to reinforce pride in personal development.

Valuing employee insights drives continuous improvement, helping organizations stay agile and aligned with their goals. Acknowledging achievements builds a sense of accomplishment, motivating employees to continue pushing for growth.

The Impact of Professional Development

Comprehensive development programs position organizations as leaders in learning and innovation, attracting top talent and retaining valuable employees. A workforce that's adaptable, resilient, and prepared for future challenges not only thrives but drives the company's progress.

Employees who are supported in their aspirations and confident in their abilities become enthusiastic ambassadors for the company's mission. They represent continuous improvement and human pride, driving the organization forward with passion and purpose.

> **Investing in professional development doesn't just prepare teams for future challenges; it creates an engaged workforce capable of extraordinary achievements.**

Investing in professional development doesn't just prepare teams for future challenges; it creates an engaged workforce capable of extraordinary achievements. This commitment goes beyond strategy—it is a declaration of the intrinsic value of every individual's potential.

Strategy Four. The Flexibility Advantage: Designing Workplaces That Adapt and Empower

As the workforce evolves, flexible work arrangements have shifted from a luxury to an absolute necessity. In today's diverse and multigenerational work environments, flexibility isn't just a perk—it's a critical foundation for balancing professional and personal priorities. This shift acknowledges the various needs of today's employees while fostering a culture of trust, pride, and engagement within organizations.

Practical flexibility allows employees to align their work with their natural rhythms and preferences. This empowerment enhances their sense of value and connection to their roles, leading to increased innovation, stronger collaboration, and a deeper commitment to organizational success.

By moving away from the rigid nine-to-five structure, companies can meet the evolving expectations of their workforce while creating an environment where everyone can thrive.

The Transformational Benefits of Flexible Work Structures

Life Balance

Flexible arrangements allow employees to integrate their work with personal commitments, such as caring for family members or attending to wellness routines. Options like remote work, flexible hours, or compressed schedules reduce stress and promote well-being. When organizations prioritize balance, they send a powerful message: they value their workforce holistically. This builds loyalty and pride, creating a foundation for long-term success.

Increased Productivity

Flexibility allows employees to work during their most productive hours and in environments that suit them, whether from home, in coworking spaces, or elsewhere. This autonomy enhances performance and fosters a culture of excellence, where employees are empowered to deliver high-quality results. Trusting employees to manage their schedules deepens their engagement with the company's mission and goals.

Talent Attraction and Retention

Millennials and Gen Z prioritize work-life integration when considering job offers. Flexible work arrangements attract top talent and help keep valuable employees by showing a company's commitment to diverse needs. Offering flexibility sends a powerful message that an organization values its people, creating a motivated, engaged workforce that's invested in the company's long-term success.

Diversity and Inclusion

Flexible work structures accommodate a wide range of employee needs, including caregivers, those with health challenges, and individuals pursuing nontraditional career paths. This inclusivity fosters creativity and problem-solving by incorporating diverse perspectives. By creating a space where everyone's contributions are valued, organizations build engagement and pride, making inclusivity a core strength that benefits all.

Improved Employee Morale

Trust is the foundation of flexibility. When employees have the autonomy to manage their work without constant oversight, morale, job satisfaction, and engagement soar. A workplace that values and respects its employees inspires motivation and fosters an environment where people excel, collaborate, and contribute to the team's success.

Health and Well-Being

Flexibility supports both physical and mental health by allowing employees to prioritize wellness activities, such as exercise, medical appointments, or taking time to recharge. This reduces burnout, fosters resilience, and creates a more creative, productive workforce. Companies that champion health and well-being demonstrate a commitment to the holistic success of their people, reinforcing employee pride and dedication.

Building a Future of Flexibility

Flexible work arrangements transform not only the individual employee experience but also boost organizational success. Empowering employees to succeed on their terms builds pride, engagement, and loyalty.

Flexibility isn't about catering to specific demographics; it's about fostering a culture of inclusivity, adaptability, and mutual trust where everyone can thrive. When employees feel supported and valued, they are more likely to innovate, collaborate, and lead with confidence.

> **Flexibility isn't about catering to specific demographics; it's about fostering a culture of inclusivity, adaptability, and mutual trust where everyone can thrive.**

By embracing flexibility, companies create dynamic, adaptable workplaces where human potential is unlocked. Flexibility isn't just a strategy—it's a pathway to collective success, where individuals and organizations grow together, leading to long-term success, creativity, and mutual achievement.

Strategy Five. Reimagining Leadership: Expanding the Definition of Success

To cultivate and elevate future leaders, organizations must rethink traditional definitions of leadership. We shouldn't measure success solely by degrees or years of experience. Instead, it should prioritize qualities like adaptability, emotional intelligence, and innovation. Embracing **diverse backgrounds** and experiences unearths hidden talents, sparks creativity, and fosters a culture of pride and progress.

This approach goes beyond the typical parameters of leadership, valuing unique contributions and empowering individuals to excel. Leadership teams that reflect the diverse makeup of their communities not only build stronger connections but also drive engagement, positioning their organizations for sustained success in today's dynamic world.

The Importance of Inclusive Leadership

Throughout my journey in retail, I've witnessed how inclusive "labor planning" sessions can shape organizational success. These discussions, evaluating roles from manager to vice president, have long emphasized equitable leadership development and representation. With tools like inclusion metrics and unconscious bias training, these efforts have enhanced fairness and aligned leadership development with organizational growth.

However, biases—whether based on gender, race, or background—have historically influenced leadership decisions.

However, biases—whether based on gender, race, or background—have historically influenced leadership decisions.

In the past, senior leaders' personal preferences sometimes overshadowed objective merit, undermining fairness and stifling innovation. Addressing these biases isn't just a matter of fairness; it's crucial for building a diverse and capable workforce, one that thrives on collaboration, creativity, and shared growth.

Why Inclusive Leadership Matters

Diverse Perspectives Fuel Innovation

Leadership that reflects a variety of backgrounds brings fresh ideas and novel approaches to problem-solving. These perspectives challenge conventional thinking, enabling organizations to adapt and thrive. Prioritizing diversity at the leadership level drives ingenuity, strengthens resilience, and ensures long-term competitiveness.

Increased Engagement and Belonging

Representation is a powerful force for connection. Employees feel inspired when they see leaders who share similar values or experiences. This sense of belonging enhances morale, fostering a culture of collaboration, engagement, and pride in the organization's mission.

Enhanced Reputation and Market Position

Inclusive leadership not only signals a commitment to equity but also drives innovation. Companies that prioritize diversity at the top are more forward-thinking, attracting top talent and cultivating loyalty among customers who align with their values. Diversity isn't just ethical; it's a strategic asset that strengthens brand positioning and trust.

Resilience in a Changing Workforce

Adaptability is key in today's evolving workforce. Leadership teams that bring diverse experiences to the table are better equipped to approach challenges imaginatively and flexibly. This adaptability enables organizations to thrive amid disruption, positioning them for sustained success and innovation.

Building an Inclusive Leadership Pipeline

Creating a leadership pipeline that reflects diversity and inclusion requires deliberate, actionable strategies.

Mentorship and Sponsorship Programs

Pairing emerging leaders with seasoned mentors fosters growth, knowledge sharing, and career advancement. These relationships empower individuals to navigate career paths with confidence and support.

Bias-Aware Evaluations

Implementing processes that mitigate unconscious bias in hiring and promotions ensures fair, merit-based decisions. These evaluations promote equity while enhancing transparency in career development.

Transparent Pathways

Developing clear career frameworks offers employees a roadmap for advancement. By creating transparent pathways, leaders can ensure equal opportunities for all, cultivating a culture where everyone has the chance to grow.

Continuous Training

Leadership development programs should prioritize inclusion, adaptability, and emotional intelligence, preparing leaders to navigate modern challenges. Continuous training reinforces organizational values and aligns leadership growth with evolving market demands.

The Transformational Power of Inclusive Leadership

By broadening leadership criteria to focus on diversity and inclusion, we create workplaces where everyone feels valued for their skills, experiences, and perspectives. Inclusive leadership fosters pride, fuels collaboration, and strengthens team bonds, driving sustained innovation and success.

Inclusive leadership fosters pride, fuels collaboration, and strengthens team bonds, driving sustained innovation and success.

It's time to rethink what leadership means. By championing inclusivity and celebrating diversity, we can build teams that inspire excellence, unlock potential, and leave a lasting impact through collective achievement. Together, we can redefine success and create a culture that values every voice and contribution.

Reflection: Leading with Inclusivity and Authenticity

Before you dive into creating actionable strategies for inclusive leadership, let's take a moment to reflect. These reflection questions help you connect with the heart of authentic leadership, guiding you toward a deeper understanding of your role in fostering inclusivity within your team.

Reflection Questions

1. **How do you show authenticity in your leadership?** Reflect on moments when you've shown vulnerability, shared your true self, or invited others to do the same. How have these actions shaped trust and collaboration within your team?

2. **How have you worked to create an inclusive environment that values diverse perspectives?** Consider whether your leadership actively fosters openness and belonging. Are there areas where voices go unheard or opportunities to make all team members feel seen and heard are missed?

3. **When was the last time you truly listened to understand rather than to respond?** Think about how active listening has deepened relationships and contributed to your team's creativity and cohesion. How can you cultivate more moments of connection and understanding?

By embracing these reflective practices, you open the door to more intentional, inclusive leadership. Let your answers guide you to shape a workplace where everyone can thrive.

KEY INSIGHTS FOR NURTURING AUTHENTIC LEADERSHIP

In today's dynamic and diverse work environment, authentic leadership has become more crucial than ever. Nurturing authenticity within your leadership approach not only inspires trust and engagement but also fosters a culture of inclusion and growth.

Prioritizing Authenticity as the Core of Leadership

Authenticity is the foundation of your leadership success. When you lead with transparency and genuineness, you allow your team to bring their full, authentic selves to work. By showing up as your true self, you inspire trust, foster open communication, and create an environment where diverse ideas can thrive. When authenticity is at the core of your leadership, every voice feels heard, respected, and valued, which cultivates a culture of pride, engagement, and mutual respect. This approach not only attracts the best talent but also strengthens loyalty and builds lasting connections. By prioritizing authenticity, you create a workplace where people feel motivated and deeply connected through shared purpose.

> **When authenticity is at the core of your leadership, every voice feels heard, respected, and valued, which cultivates a culture of pride, engagement, and mutual respect.**

Embracing Inclusivity for Greater Collaboration

Inclusivity is a vital practice that empowers your team to reach its full potential. When you get ideas from different people, you can be more creative and come up with better solutions. When you encourage diverse voices, you ensure that everyone can contribute ideas that shape the organization's direction. As a result, problem-solving becomes more effective and decision-making improves. Creating an inclusive environment means you value everyone's ideas, leading to stronger collaborations and a deeper sense of pride in the collective effort. This environment of empowerment fosters innovation, fueling organizational success and creating a shared passion and purpose within your team.

Empowering Through
Intentional Leadership Practices

Your leadership journey requires adaptability and an understanding of your team's evolving needs. By leading with intention, you focus on actively listening and recalibrating strategies to address challenges and aspirations with purpose. Offering personalized support allows you to show your commitment to their growth. When you take the time to tailor your approach to each individual's needs, you show that their contributions matter and that you are invested in their success. This builds trust and strengthens their sense of pride. Leading intentionally fosters an atmosphere of encouragement and shared accountability, where everyone works toward collective success.

Measuring Impact to Drive Meaningful Change

Progress must be measurable to drive real and sustained change. By establishing clear metrics for inclusivity and equity, you can track your progress, uncover gaps, and celebrate milestones. Measuring inclusion allows you to ensure your efforts are making an impact and helps you refine your strategies to meet the evolving needs of your workforce. When you actively track and celebrate progress, your team will feel more connected and empowered, knowing their contributions are helping shape the organization's culture. This transparency fosters accountability, reinforces pride, and ensures inclusivity becomes ingrained in your leadership style.

Creating Opportunities for Growth and Development

Professional development reflects your commitment to your team's growth. When you provide personalized development opportunities—such as tailored growth plans or inclusive leadership training—you empower individuals to take charge of their future. By aligning their growth with the organization's goals, you ensure each person's career trajectory supports both personal aspirations and company objectives. These opportunities nurture upward mobility, resilience, and innovation, reinforcing a sense of pride in their progress. When you invest in your team's growth, you prepare them to face the future with confidence and the skills to meet new challenges.

By embracing these principles, you can create a workplace where inclusivity, authenticity, and empowerment are foundational to success. When you lead with authenticity, prioritize inclusivity, and provide opportunities for growth, you foster an environment where people feel valued, supported, and connected. This drives collaboration, ignites innovation, and ensures shared success within your team and organization.

YOUR NEXT STEPS:
INSPIRING CONNECTION AND BELONGING

Authenticity and inclusivity are the foundational pillars that support transformative leadership. As a leader, your commitment to fostering these principles will shape a workplace where pride, collaboration, and innovation can flourish. By embodying these values, you create an environment where everyone feels seen, heard, and empowered.

1. Lead with Authenticity

Authenticity creates trust and fosters meaningful communication.

▶ Share your values, vision, and mission with your team so they understand not just what you do but why you do it.

- ▶ Encourage open and honest dialogue, ensuring everyone feels safe and respected to express themselves.

Action Step: Reflect on a personal experience that shaped your leadership style and share it with your team. Use this as an opportunity to connect with them on a deeper level and model how authenticity can drive a culture of trust.

2. Champion Inclusivity

Inclusivity unlocks innovation and drives effective collaboration.

- ▶ Actively seek diverse perspectives and voices within your team to create a richer, more creative environment.
- ▶ Address unconscious biases through training, intentional recruitment practices, and creating a workplace where everyone feels welcome.

Action Step: Identify one area of inclusivity in your team or organization that needs improvement (e.g., recruitment, meetings, promotions) and create an action plan to tackle it. Involve your team in this process to ensure solutions reflect diverse perspectives.

3. Empower Growth Through Development

Fostering growth empowers your team to take pride in their contributions and inspire lasting success.

- ▶ Provide tailored opportunities for learning and development to help individuals grow in their unique career paths.
- ▶ Regularly celebrate progress and milestones to reinforce the value of continuous improvement.

Action Step: Collaborate with your team to create personalized development plans. Identify one new skill or area of interest for each team member and provide them with resources to support their growth.

4. Measure and Celebrate Belonging

Metrics are essential to understanding where you are and where you need to go in terms of inclusivity.

- Regularly track key inclusion metrics, such as diversity in recruitment, retention rates, and employee satisfaction.
- Use these data insights to adjust your strategies and celebrate the progress made toward creating an inclusive culture.

Action Step: Launch an inclusivity survey to collect employee feedback on workplace culture and areas for improvement. Share the results openly with your team and use the feedback to guide further initiatives.

5. Embrace Flexibility

Flexibility promotes well-being and engagement, allowing employees to thrive both personally and professionally.

- To accommodate diverse needs, offer flexible work options like remote work or flexible hours.
- Empower employees to take ownership of their time and productivity, demonstrating trust and respect for their work-life balance.

Action Step: Implement a pilot program for flexible work arrangements within your team. Gather feedback on its impact and explore how to optimize it for long-term success.

Your Leadership Impact

Leadership rooted in authenticity and inclusivity is not just about managing—it's about creating an environment where pride, engagement, and collaboration can thrive. By prioritizing these principles, you invite your team to bring their entire selves to work, creating a workplace built on trust, innovation, and shared success.

> **Now is the time for you to lead with heart and intention, setting the stage for a legacy of inclusivity and authenticity that propels extraordinary outcomes.**

Now is the time for you to lead with heart and intention, setting the stage for a legacy of inclusivity and authenticity that propels extraordinary outcomes. By unlocking the full potential and pride of every individual, you'll foster a team that is engaged, motivated, and ready to redefine what success looks like in your organization.

Career development becomes less about rigid pathways and more about unlocking potential, exploring passions, and building supportive relationships.

CHAPTER 7

GENERATIONAL HARMONY

Building Inclusive Leadership for a Multigenerational Workforce

From the wisdom of baby boomers to the tech-savvy ingenuity of Gen Z, each generation offers unique insights that enrich collaboration, innovation, and the collective potential of a workforce.

A decade ago, I found myself entrenched in what I now realize was a narrow "boomer mindset." I believed that refining my leadership style would automatically resonate with everyone I worked with. Writing this book and reflecting on my journey illuminated a profound truth: authentic leadership is not about perfecting a one-size-fits-all approach. Instead, it thrives on empathy, curiosity, and adaptability. In today's multigenerational workplaces, the era of universal solutions has passed.

> In today's multigenerational workplaces, the era of universal solutions has passed.

Regardless of your industry, success depends on understanding and celebrating the diverse strengths of your workforce. **Inclusive leadership**, rooted in flexibility and attentiveness, ensures everyone feels seen, valued, and motivated to excel. This inclusivity not only fosters innovation but also strengthens relationships, creating environments where shared goals and deeper connections flourish.

What is the most fulfilling aspect? Embracing generational differences unlocks both personal and collective growth. Valuing people's contributions makes them more engaged, proud of their work, and striving for excellence. Your commitment to inclusivity serves as a catalyst for individual and team potential, driving achievements that benefit everyone.

This chapter delves into the importance of adaptability in leadership, especially in a workforce as diverse as today's. By leveraging the strengths of each generation, leaders can foster collaboration, encourage creativity, and maintain innovation as a cornerstone of success.

GENERATIONAL DYNAMICS: UNDERSTANDING THE DIFFERENCES

The adage "Age is more than just a number" encapsulates the richness of generational dynamics in the workplace. Age, shaped by lived experiences, influences how people collaborate, communicate, and pursue their goals. While it's essential to avoid reductive stereotypes, each generation contributes distinct strengths influenced by the times they've lived through:

> ▶ **Traditionalists** and **baby boomers** bring a wealth of wisdom, loyalty, and a deep appreciation for long-term relationships.

Their emphasis on stability and dedication creates a grounding presence in the workplace.

- **Gen X** excels in balancing personal and professional responsibilities, thriving in flexible, evolving environments. Their resilience and adaptability, honed during technological transitions, make them practical problem-solvers.
- **Millennials** prioritize purpose-driven work, personal growth, and social responsibility. Their focus on open communication and collaboration fosters inclusivity and drives positive cultural change.
- **Gen Z** is defined by authenticity, inclusivity, and a strong desire for meaningful contributions. As digital natives, they challenge the status quo with their innovative thinking and openness to change.

Understanding these generational characteristics allows leaders to leverage their strengths effectively, building bridges across diverse perspectives to drive collective success.

Understanding these generational characteristics allows leaders to leverage their strengths effectively, building bridges across diverse perspectives to drive collective success.

BUILDING BRIDGES ACROSS GENERATIONS

We should not view generational differences as obstacles but as opportunities to create synergy. Each generation offers distinct strengths that can form an incredibly resilient and innovative workforce. Leadership in today's diverse workplace means acting as a bridge builder, creating pathways for communication and understanding across age groups.

Why is this so important? A **multigenerational workforce** represents a living mosaic of experiences, perspectives, and skills. Each generation's unique context shapes its contributions, and their harmonious combination provides a competitive edge in today's dynamic marketplace. Ignoring or downplaying these differences risks fostering misunderstanding or division, which can lead to decreased engagement, innovation, and overall morale. Conversely, celebrating generational diversity creates a culture of inclusion where employees feel valued and motivated to bring their best ideas forward.

> **A multigenerational workforce represents a living mosaic of experiences, perspectives, and skills.**

Building these bridges also prepares organizations for long-term resilience. In a changing world, adaptability is key, and leveraging the strengths of every generation equips teams to navigate uncertainty with agility and confidence. Baby boomers' strategic vision complements Millennials' technological savvy, while Gen Z's innovation energizes the practicality of Gen X. By embracing this interplay of skills and approaches, companies position themselves not just to survive but to thrive, creating a foundation of collaboration and creativity that drives both immediate and sustained success.

When leaders actively bridge the generational gap, they unlock the collective potential of their teams, driving not just performance but a culture of mutual pride and purpose. Together, these efforts result in a workplace where everyone, regardless of their age, thrives and feels integral to the organization's mission.

UNDERSTANDING AND LEADING GEN Z

Often misunderstood, Gen Z (born mid-1990s to early 2010s) represents a generation of forward-thinking changemakers. Despite occasional criticism, they bring immense potential to workplaces by driving inclusivity, creativity, and purpose-driven practices.

With two billion members globally, Gen Z now outnumbers baby boomers. However, research reveals that 40 percent of leaders perceive them as underprepared for the workforce. Misunderstanding often stems from traditional expectations clashing with Gen Z's awareness of their unique strengths. While they may lack conventional experience, they excel in digital fluency, collaboration, and adaptability—qualities critical in today's fast-changing landscape.

Shaped by transformative global events, such as the COVID-19 pandemic and movements for social justice, Gen Z prioritizes purpose-driven work aligned with their values. They emphasize balance, flexibility, and opportunities to contribute substantially.

The most exciting part? Gen Z thrives in environments that encourage creativity and innovation. When leaders provide spaces for them to share ideas and take ownership of their work, Gen Z emerges as an invaluable asset, shaping the future of the workplace.

By recognizing and embracing Gen Z's strengths, leaders foster inclusive cultures prepared to address challenges and drive long-term success.

LEADING A MULTIGENERATIONAL WORKFORCE

In the following sections, you will explore actionable strategies for navigating the complexities of a multigenerational workforce. By fostering adaptability and inclusivity, leaders can inspire creativity, build collaboration, and create environments where everyone can thrive.

You'll uncover how to unlock the extraordinary potential of a workforce enriched by generational diversity, transforming challenges into opportunities for innovation and success.

Reflection: Tuning into the Richness of Generational Diversity

Before diving into actionable strategies, let's take a moment to reflect on the profound opportunities that arise from leading a multigenerational workforce. Reflection allows us to connect with our values and intentions, helping us understand how we can foster an environment where **generational diversity** is not just acknowledged but celebrated. It's an opportunity to pause and consider how our leadership can bridge differences, spark collaboration, and unleash collective potential.

> **Generational diversity is a powerful asset, offering a spectrum of perspectives, experiences, and skills.**

Generational diversity is a powerful asset, offering a spectrum of perspectives, experiences, and skills. Yet harnessing this potential requires curiosity, empathy, and an unwavering commitment to inclusivity. Reflection is where this journey begins—illuminating our assumptions, revealing opportunities for growth, and guiding us toward meaningful action.

Here are three thought-provoking questions to help you explore your role in fostering generational harmony and leveraging the unique strengths of your workforce:

1. **How do you bridge generational gaps within your team?** Reflect on the moments when you've actively fostered understanding and connection between colleagues of different generations. What strategies have been most effective? Where might there still be opportunities to strengthen these relationships?

2. **In what ways do you embrace and celebrate the unique strengths each generation brings to your workplace?** Consider how you recognize and amplify the contributions of your team members, from baby boomers' strategic foresight to Gen Z's innovative spirit. Are there new ways to align these diverse talents toward shared goals?

3. **How do your generational experiences shape your leadership style?** Explore how your perspective, shaped by your generation, influences your decisions and interactions. Are there biases or blind spots limiting your ability to fully embrace the strengths of other generations?

As you ponder these questions, allow yourself to lean into curiosity and openness. Reflection is not about judgment but about discovery—a chance to see where you stand and where you can grow. By starting here, you set the foundation for leadership that bridges divides, elevates collaboration, and transforms generational diversity into a powerful force for innovation and success.

ADAPT FOR SUCCESS: FIVE FUNDAMENTALS FOR MULTIGENERATIONAL LEADERSHIP

Leading a multigenerational workforce requires understanding and adapting to the unique strengths and perspectives each generation brings. Here are five fundamental strategies to help you navigate and leverage this diversity for organizational success.

Fundamental One. Tailored Beginnings: Recruitment and Onboarding for a Multigenerational Workforce

Understanding how generational differences shape workplace pride is crucial during recruitment and onboarding. Each generation brings unique motivations and expectations rooted in their life experiences and societal contexts. Recognizing these distinctions early enables leaders to develop **customized strategies** that foster meaningful connections, paving the way for lasting engagement and success.

Recruitment: Appealing to Diverse Motivations

Generational priorities for selecting roles differ widely. Younger candidates often seek innovation, flexibility, and opportunities for meaningful contributions, while seasoned professionals may prioritize stability, comprehensive benefits, and alignment with personal values. Crafting job descriptions that emphasize career growth and purpose attracts younger applicants, while highlighting reliability and advancement opportunities resonate with more experienced candidates. Authentic messaging that reflects these priorities draws a diverse, engaged talent pool.

As a co-founder of a retail recruiting company, I've observed how automated hiring tools can overlook talent. Digital platforms and

AI-driven systems streamline processes but often cannot capture the depth of experience seasoned candidates bring. Algorithms may prioritize keywords and metrics, filtering out invaluable skills. Automation can alienate candidates who prefer personalized interactions, diminishing their connection to the hiring process.

Strategies for Embracing Generational Diversity in Recruitment

- ▶ **Tailored Interview Questions:** While standard questions ensure fairness, they may not reveal generational strengths. Younger candidates excel when discussing innovation and collaboration, while experienced professionals shine in mentorship and leadership. Customizing questions based on values uncover meaningful insights.
- ▶ **Highlight Workplace Priorities:** Showcase core values like sustainability and diversity for younger candidates and emphasize stability and growth opportunities for seasoned professionals. This alignment shows your commitment to understanding diverse priorities.
- ▶ **Flexible Interview Options:** Offering in-person and virtual formats accommodates different preferences, creating a welcoming experience. While seasoned candidates may prefer face-to-face interactions, virtual options often appeal to younger applicants.
- ▶ **Inclusive Candidate Engagement:** Including team members from various generations in interviews provides candidates with a fuller view of the workplace, fostering rapport and demonstrating collaboration.
- ▶ **Personalized Communication:** Tailored follow-ups referencing specific interview points show respect and attention to detail, setting your company apart and conveying genuine care for potential hires.

Onboarding: Cultivating Belonging Through Generational Sensitivity

Onboarding plays a pivotal role in fostering pride and facilitating smooth transitions. Programs tailored to generational preferences, such as addressing Gen Z's tech fluency or acknowledging baby boomers' expertise, help new hires feel supported and valued from day one.

Customizing training to accommodate different technical proficiencies and learning styles speeds up integration and boosts confidence. This attentiveness fosters belonging and motivation, laying the groundwork for long-term engagement.

Key Onboarding Strategies

- **Inclusive Training Materials:** Design resources that address diverse learning preferences, ensuring all team members have access to essential tools for success.
- **Mentorship Across Generations:** Pair new hires with mentors from different generational backgrounds to encourage knowledge sharing and build connections.
- **Optional Technology Workshops:** Offer sessions to familiarize employees with workplace systems, catering to varying levels of tech comfort.
- **Early Milestone Recognition:** Celebrate initial achievements to build confidence and reinforce a sense of accomplishment.

Why It Matters

Tailored recruitment and onboarding strategies go beyond attracting talent—they inspire pride and build lasting connections. When new hires feel understood and supported, they become motivated contributors aligned with your company's vision and mission.

By respecting generational diversity and demonstrating thoughtful care, you create a workplace culture that values every contribution. This approach enhances retention, fosters loyalty, and establishes a strong foundation for sustained success, preparing your team to tackle challenges and achieve extraordinary outcomes.

By respecting generational diversity and demonstrating thoughtful care, you create a workplace culture that values every contribution.

Fundamental Two. Evaluating with Purpose: Redefining Performance Reviews for Inclusivity

As recruitment and onboarding adapt to diverse teams, performance evaluations must also evolve to reflect inclusivity and personalization. Historically, standardized frameworks prioritized uniformity, simplifying processes for leaders and HR professionals. However, these systems often overlooked the unique strengths, values, and motivations that distinguish employees across generations, leaving potential untapped and growth opportunities missed.

In a multigenerational workforce, meaningful evaluations are powerful tools for fostering engagement, morale, and

By embracing generational differences, leaders can transform routine reviews into personalized, impactful experiences that inspire employees to excel.

productivity. By embracing generational differences, leaders can transform routine reviews into personalized, impactful experiences that inspire employees to excel.

Each generation brings unique strengths shaped by historical and cultural contexts. Ignoring these nuances risks disengagement, reduced morale, and underutilized talent. Leaders who adopt **inclusive evaluation practices** create environments where feedback is constructive, resonant, and empowering.

Generational Approaches to Feedback

- ▶ **Baby boomers:** Value structured, goal-oriented evaluations that highlight long-term contributions and align future goals with company priorities. Recognizing their achievements reinforces dedication and professional pride.
- ▶ **Millennials** and **Gen Z:** Thrive on real-time feedback and collaborative discussions. These groups seek regular, actionable input to adapt and grow. Digital tools and frequent check-ins ensure sustained engagement.

Personalizing feedback across generations may seem challenging, but the following strategies make it seamless and impactful.

Key Strategies for Inclusive Performance Reviews

1. Flexible Feedback Schedules

Adopt a hybrid feedback model combining formal annual reviews with informal check-ins to meet diverse preferences.

- ▶ **Annual Reviews:** Provide in-depth reflections on achievements, career goals, and long-term aspirations.
- ▶ **Informal Check-Ins:** Address immediate challenges and celebrate wins to ensure ongoing support.

This dual approach balances the structure valued by seasoned professionals with the continuous feedback sought by younger employees.

2. Personalized Development Plans

Collaborate with employees to design career-growth plans tailored to their stages and aspirations.

- ▶ **For Early-Career Professionals:** Emphasize skill building and learning opportunities.
- ▶ **For Seasoned Employees:** Highlight mentorship roles and strategic initiatives.

Personalized plans show leadership's investment in growth, aligning employee ambitions with organizational goals and fostering pride and loyalty.

3. Leveraging Technology for Feedback

Using digital platforms to deliver real-time feedback and track progress appeals to tech-savvy Millennials and Gen Z while streamlining communication for others.

- ▶ **Recognition Apps:** Facilitate instant acknowledgment of achievements.
- ▶ **Progress Dashboards:** Visualize goals and milestones to enhance ownership and accountability.

Technology-driven tools foster transparency and responsiveness, empowering employees to engage actively in their development.

4. Mentorship Programs

Pair employees across generations to foster skill sharing and collaboration.

- ▶ **Outcomes:** Build mutual respect, enhance team creativity, and strengthen intergenerational relationships.

Mentorship transforms generational differences into opportunities for collective growth, driving trust and innovation.

5. Diverse Feedback Channels

Offer multiple avenues for feedback delivery, such as face-to-face conversations, emails, or digital tools, to accommodate varied communication preferences.

> ▶ **Why It Works:** Personalized communication ensures inclusivity and shows leadership's adaptability.

When employees feel heard, they are more likely to act on feedback and remain committed to their roles.

Transforming Evaluations into Growth Opportunities

Reimagining performance evaluations isn't just about updating processes; it's about aligning them with the diversity of today's workforce. Tailored methods inspire pride, engagement, and belonging, turning feedback into a driver of success.

> **Reimagining performance evaluations isn't just about updating processes; it's about aligning them with the diversity of today's workforce.**

Employees empowered by meaningful evaluations are more motivated to innovate, collaborate, and excel. This inclusive approach enhances individual contributions while propelling the company toward extraordinary outcomes.

Takeaway: Performance evaluations are more than procedural tasks—they're opportunities to celebrate achievements, inspire growth, and build a culture where recognition thrives. By embracing inclusivity and personalization, you unlock potential across generations, creating a workforce ready to achieve remarkable success.

Fundamental Three. Bridging Differences: Turning Generational Conflict into Collaboration

Generational differences shape workplace interactions and how people approach conflicts. These variations influence team dynamics, employees' sense of pride, and their connection to the organization. When managed well, generational disparities in **conflict resolution** can become opportunities for collaboration, relationship building, and team cohesion.

> **When managed well, generational disparities in conflict resolution can become opportunities for collaboration, relationship building, and team cohesion.**

Generational Approaches to Conflict Resolution

Younger generations, especially Millennials and Gen Z, value direct engagement and open dialogue. They prioritize transparent conversations and swift resolutions, aligning with their preference for immediacy and candid conversations. This approach fosters innovation and prevents issues from lingering. If mishandled, their directness may seem blunt or confrontational to others.

In contrast, older generations, like baby boomers, often prefer diplomacy and tactful communication, shaped by more hierarchical and formal work environments. Their conflict style emphasizes harmony and compromise, which helps avoid escalation but can leave underlying issues unresolved.

These differing styles can lead to misunderstandings. Younger employees might view indirect communication as avoidance, while seasoned professionals may interpret directness as aggression. Left unaddressed, these dynamics can erode trust, hinder collaboration, and weaken team effectiveness.

The Benefits of Embracing Generational Differences

Harnessing Diverse Problem-Solving Strengths

Each generation brings unique strategies to conflict resolution. Younger employees excel at addressing challenges head-on and driving innovation, while older colleagues provide thoughtful, diplomatic solutions. Combining these strengths enables teams to tackle conflicts with a balanced approach, yielding more effective outcomes.

This synergy transforms differences into assets, equipping teams with a comprehensive toolkit for navigating challenges and fostering adaptability and creativity.

Building Mutual Respect and Belonging

Addressing generational differences fosters understanding and respect. Valuing employees' perspectives encourages constructive engagement, building trust and a sense of belonging.

By valuing diverse conflict-resolution styles, organizations create a culture of inclusivity and unity, strengthening collaboration and aligning teams toward shared goals.

Strategies to Bridge Generational Conflict

Facilitate Generational Workshops

Host workshops that explore and celebrate diverse conflict-resolution styles.

> **Benefits:** Encourages open discussions, builds mutual respect, and fosters empathy

Practice Conflict Resolution Skills

Engage teams in simulations showcasing diverse approaches to conflict.

> **Why It Works:** Provides a safe space for understanding alternative strategies and builds confidence for real-world situations

Structured Feedback Sessions

Hold regular feedback sessions to discuss communication preferences and conflict styles.

> **Impact:** Helps younger employees advocate for transparency while allowing older colleagues to highlight the value of diplomacy

Cross-Generational Mentorship

To exchange insights on conflict resolution, pair employees from different generations.

> **Outcome:** Younger employees share direct engagement techniques, while seasoned professionals impart tactful communication skills.

Develop a Communication Charter

Create a team-wide charter outlining agreed methods for addressing conflicts.

Transforming Conflict into Collaboration

Generational differences, when understood and embraced, can strengthen teams and enhance collaboration. Ignoring these variations risks tension and disengagement, but addressing them creates opportunities for trust and innovation.

By fostering dialogue, promoting respect, and leveraging diverse strengths, leaders can build a culture where collaboration thrives. This approach ensures every team member feels valued and empowered to contribute their best.

Takeaway: Generational differences are not barriers—they are catalysts for growth and success. With intentional leadership, these differences become assets that drive innovation, deepen connections, and create a thriving workplace.

Fundamental Four. Embracing Change Together: Building Resilience Across Generations

Change is inevitable in any thriving workplace, but it often brings challenges that test **resilience** and adaptability. Shifting routines and confronting uncertainty can evoke resistance, especially in a multigenerational workforce where each generation brings unique perspectives and coping styles.

> **Change is inevitable in any thriving workplace, but it often brings challenges that test resilience and adaptability.**

Older employees often approach change with caution, relying on experience and proven methods to navigate uncertainty. Their long-term perspective acts as a stabilizing force during transitions. Meanwhile, younger colleagues see change as a gateway to innovation and growth, embracing new ideas with enthusiasm. These differences can create friction but also offer opportunities to harness diverse strengths and foster collective resilience.

Leaders who embrace these dynamics can create a culture that respects individuality while aligning efforts toward shared goals. By encouraging open collaboration and addressing differences, they can transform resistance into growth, fostering trust, pride, and adaptability.

Why Resilience Matters in a Multigenerational Workforce

Harnessing Diverse Strengths

The reflective approaches of older employees balance the energy and willingness to experiment with their younger colleagues. Together, these perspectives create well-rounded strategies for tackling challenges.

Valuing diverse contributions builds trust, strengthens decision-making, and equips teams to face uncertainty with confidence. Resilience becomes a collective strength, enabling teams to adapt and excel.

Valuing diverse contributions builds trust, strengthens decision-making, and equips teams to face uncertainty with confidence.

Fostering Engagement Through Shared Purpose

When employees from all generations feel their input is valued, they engage more deeply in change initiatives. This shared investment inspires pride and strengthens connections.

Resilient teams approach challenges as opportunities, driven by a collective purpose. Leaders who prioritize inclusivity during transitions cultivate a sense of belonging, fueling collaboration and innovation.

Strategies for Leading Resilient Change

- ▶ **Inclusive Change Committees:** Form committees with representatives from all generations to guide transitions.
  - ★ **Why It Works:** Diverse perspectives uncover hidden challenges and opportunities, while inclusion fosters trust and ownership.
  - ★ **Impact:** Strategies become more comprehensive and align with the workforce's diverse needs.
- ▶ **Tailored Training Programs:** Design initiatives that address generational learning preferences.
  - ★ **Examples:** Older employees may prefer in-person workshops, while younger colleagues thrive in interactive online modules.
  - ★ **Benefits:** Employees feel supported and confident, reinforcing pride and capability across the team.
- ▶ **Mentorship for Change:** Pair experienced employees with younger colleagues to navigate transitions together.
  - ★ **Why It Works:** Seasoned professionals offer stability and context, while younger participants bring fresh perspectives and enthusiasm.
  - ★ **Outcome:** Strengthened relationships turn change into a shared journey.
- ▶ **Feedback Loops During Transitions:** Implement regular feedback channels, such as surveys or team discussions, to gather input.
  - ★ **How It Helps:** This ensures everyone can speak and promotes respect.
  - ★ **Impact:** Transparent adjustments build trust and a collaborative culture.

- ▶ **Recognizing Adaptability:** Celebrate individuals or teams who embrace change.
  - ★ **Why It Matters:** Public recognition motivates others to view change positively.
  - ★ **Outcome:** Highlighting success stories reinforces a culture of resilience and optimism.

Building a Culture of Resilience

Navigating change in a multigenerational workforce requires thoughtful leadership rooted in communication, collaboration, and adaptability. Leaders who value diversity and inclusivity create environments where employees feel respected, engaged, and empowered to thrive.

By fostering trust, providing tailored support, and recognizing achievements, change becomes a uniting force that inspires collective pride and success. Organizations and their people can endure uncertainty and grow stronger together.

The takeaway: Change is an opportunity to unite and excel. Inclusive strategies transform differences into strengths, creating a resilient workforce ready to tackle any challenge.

The takeaway: Change is an opportunity to unite and excel.

Fundamental Five. Cultivating Careers: Conversations That Ignite Growth Across Generations

"How do you see your career evolving?" This modern twist on the classic "Where do you see yourself in three to five years?" underscores the transformative power of **career development**

conversations. These discussions go beyond setting goals—they build bridges that foster pride, loyalty, and motivation across generations.

For younger professionals, these conversations spark excitement about acquiring new skills, tackling challenges, and exploring advancement opportunities. They see them as guidance sessions to help chart a path toward their aspirations. Seasoned professionals often view these dialogues as chances to refine expertise, mentor others, and align their roles with cherished values. Tailoring these conversations to diverse generational perspectives ensures employees feel valued, respected, and inspired.

A thoughtful dialogue has a significant impact. For younger colleagues, leaders might ask, "What skills do you want to master for exciting future opportunities?" For experienced team members, consider honoring their legacy with a question like "What areas of your expertise would you like to expand or share?" Personalized approaches like these strengthen trust and respect, instilling pride in employees' unique journeys.

When leaders prioritize career conversations, they foster a culture of inclusivity, collaboration, and innovation. A single meaningful conversation can inspire an employee's sense of purpose, motivating them to take ownership of their growth. Career development becomes less about rigid pathways and more about unlocking potential, exploring passions, and building supportive relationships.

> **Career development becomes less about rigid pathways and more about unlocking potential, exploring passions, and building supportive relationships.**

The Value of Career Conversations

▶ **Empowering Employees to Own Their Growth:** Career development isn't about imposing paths; it's about equipping people with the tools to define and pursue their success. Employees who feel heard in these conversations are more likely to take ownership of their trajectories, fostering deeper engagement, loyalty, and pride in their contributions.

▶ **Building a Culture of Trust and Inclusivity:** Leaders who invest in these dialogues signal genuine commitment to their team's growth. Employees feel valued, whether they seek rapid skill acquisition or focus on legacy-building. This inclusivity strengthens bonds, reduces turnover, and nurtures a shared sense of purpose.

Strategies for Meaningful Career Conversations

Individual Development Plans (IDPs)

Encourage team members to create personalized plans outlining goals, skills, and growth activities.

▶ **Why It Works:** Tailored plans respect individual aspirations while offering a clear growth roadmap.

▶ **Impact:** IDPs empower employees, align ambitions with organizational goals, and enhance commitment and retention.

Regular Career Check-ins

Schedule consistent one-on-one conversations about aspirations, skill building, and future opportunities.

▶ **Why It Works:** Focusing on growth over metrics fosters trust and reinforces support.

▶ **Impact:** Check-ins build morale, encourage open communication, and ensure employees feel valued.

Skill Development Workshops

Offer workshops that address the diverse needs of a multigenerational workforce.

- ▶ **Examples:**
  - ★ Younger colleagues: Digital fluency, creative problem-solving
  - ★ Seasoned professionals: Advanced leadership, strategic planning
- ▶ **Impact:** Boosts confidence, demonstrates the company's commitment to growth, and ensures all employees feel supported.

Career Pathway Mapping

Host sessions to help employees visualize career trajectories and identify key skills for advancement.

- ▶ **Why It Works:** Highlighting clear pathways reinforces the company's dedication to success.
- ▶ **Impact:** Inspires motivation, aligns aspirations with goals, and strengthens loyalty.

Peer Networking Opportunities

Facilitate cross-departmental events where colleagues share experiences and insights.

- ▶ **Why It Works:** Networking broadens perspectives, builds community, and opens doors to opportunities.
- ▶ **Impact:** Encourages innovation, strengthens collaboration, and cultivates pride in the workplace.

The Bottom Line

Career conversations are powerful tools for creating workplaces where people feel valued and inspired to grow. Engaging in meaningful dialogues unlocks team potential and builds a culture where pride and achievement thrive.

Prioritizing these conversations shows a commitment to valuing diverse aspirations and fostering growth for all. The result? A dynamic, innovative environment where employees are motivated to contribute their best and are prepared to embrace the future with confidence.

PRINCIPLES FOR MULTIGENERATIONAL LEADERSHIP EXCELLENCE

In today's diverse workplace, it's crucial for leaders to embrace the unique strengths and perspectives of multiple generations. By fostering a welcoming environment, you can make sure everyone feels valued and motivated. This section will explore key principles for leveraging generational diversity to drive innovation and growth.

Recognize the Value of Diverse Perspectives

To harness the distinct strengths and experiences that each generation brings to the workplace, you must create an environment where every voice contributes to richer, more innovative outcomes. By appreciating generational differences, you foster a culture of inclusion, respect, and collaboration. Acknowledging the unique life experiences of each generation encourages a deeper sense of belonging, which increases motivation and creativity. This recognition not only strengthens your team's sense of pride but also drives loyalty and engagement.

Adapt Leadership Approaches for Inclusivity

As a leader, you must evolve from a one-size-fits-all approach to one that is flexible and empathetic. Tailoring your leadership style ensures that every team member, regardless of age or experience, feels seen, valued, and supported in their professional journey. By adapting your leadership to meet diverse needs, you build trust and create a cohesive team that can work seamlessly across generational differences. This approach helps you cultivate a culture of equity, empowering each individual to contribute their best and positioning your organization for long-term success in an ever-changing world.

Leverage Generational Strengths for Collective Growth

You can amplify your team's capacity to address challenges and seize opportunities by aligning the strengths of each generation. Recognize and leverage the wisdom of baby boomers, the adaptability of Gen X, the collaboration of Millennials, and the innovation of Gen Z. When you create opportunities for cross-generational collaboration, you promote knowledge-sharing and mentorship that accelerates problem-solving and drives innovation. These efforts not only enhance individual growth but also build resilience, strengthening your team's overall performance and success.

Foster Open Communication and Mutual Understanding

Prioritizing open communication is key to bridging generational gaps and building mutual respect. Proactive dialogue reduces misunderstandings, encourages collaboration, and strengthens workplace cohesion. Establishing clear frameworks for constructive conversations and conflict resolution enhances team dynamics and fosters an inclusive environment. When you lead these discussions, you show your commitment to inclusivity, which boosts morale and inspires trust. Eventually, this approach creates a space where diverse perspectives are celebrated and every team member feels valued and heard.

Create Pathways for Growth and Shared Success

Empower your team by offering opportunities for learning, mentorship, and career development across all age groups. When you provide clear pathways for advancement and skill building, you encourage individuals to reach their full potential while contributing to broader organizational goals. Celebrating individual and team achievements instills pride and drives sustained excellence. These growth opportunities prepare your team for future challenges and build a skilled, adaptable workforce aligned with your vision. By aligning individual growth with shared success, you ensure your team remains engaged and committed to achieving collective goals.

By recognizing the unique strengths of each generation and tailoring your leadership strategies to empower, celebrate, and bridge generational differences, you create a dynamic, resilient, and innovative workforce that thrives on collaboration and shared success. This leadership approach fosters an inclusive culture where pride and engagement propel your team toward extraordinary outcomes.

YOUR NEXT STEPS:
LEADING ACROSS GENERATIONS

A multigenerational workforce presents unique challenges and opportunities, offering a dynamic environment where diverse perspectives fuel innovation and growth. By prioritizing empathy, flexibility, and shared goals, leaders can create workplaces where every generation feels valued and motivated to excel.

1. Foster Empathy Across Generations

Empathy is the cornerstone of inclusive leadership.

- ▶ Understand and respect the diverse experiences, values, and communication styles of each generation.
- ▶ Adapt your approach to accommodate their unique needs and preferences.

Action Step: Host a generational workshop where team members share their workplace values and experiences. Use this as an opportunity to foster mutual understanding and build stronger connections.

2. Customize Communication for Clarity

Tailored communication ensures engagement and trust.

- ▶ Adjust your communication style to resonate with the preferences of each generation.
- ▶ Use formal updates for seasoned professionals and concise digital formats for younger team members.

Action Step: Survey your team to identify their preferred communication methods. Implement changes that cater to these preferences, ensuring everyone feels included and engaged.

3. Embrace Flexibility

Flexibility empowers people to perform at their best:

- ▶ Offer hybrid work models, tailored training programs, and adaptable workflows.

- Recognize the unique needs of each generation to foster pride and engagement.

Action Step: Pilot a flexible work initiative that allows employees to customize their schedules or workflows. Collect feedback to improve and expand the program.

4. Align Around Shared Goals

Shared objectives bridge generational gaps and encourage collaboration.

- Create opportunities for cross-generational projects that highlight individual strengths.
- Foster teamwork by aligning everyone around shared goals and celebrating shared successes.

Action Step: Launch a cross-functional project team with members from diverse age groups. Define shared objectives and encourage regular collaboration to build trust and unity.

5. Recognize and Celebrate Contributions

Recognition drives engagement and reinforces a culture of appreciation.

- Adapt recognition methods to each generation's preferences, ranging from formal awards to public acknowledgments.
- Celebrate milestones and achievements to inspire pride and motivation.

Action Step: Establish a recognition program that highlights contributions from all team members. Rotate recognition formats to appeal to diverse preferences and ensure inclusivity.

YOUR LEADERSHIP LEGACY

Leading across generations requires empathy, adaptability, and a commitment to inclusivity. By recognizing and leveraging the unique strengths of each age group, you create a thriving, innovative workplace where collaboration and engagement flourish.

> **By recognizing and leveraging the unique strengths of each age group, you create a thriving, innovative workplace where collaboration and engagement flourish.**

As you implement these strategies, remember that authentic leadership is a continuous journey. Embrace the opportunity to learn from your team, adapt to their needs, and inspire their best work.

Together, you'll build a multigenerational workforce that thrives on shared purpose, respect, and collective success.

Leading in a collaborative environment is less about authority and more about creating space for others to excel.

CHAPTER 8

LEADING WITHOUT TITLES

Inspiring Change and Impact at Any Level

If you haven't done so today, take a moment to reflect on the strength you already possess and the profound influence you carry. Leadership transcends titles—it thrives in the moments where your actions inspire, your energy uplifts, and your vision ignites change. Every interaction, idea, and effort you make has the potential to impact lives, elevate relationships, and drive meaningful progress. Recognizing this power is the first step toward embracing the boundless opportunities around you.

Think of yourself as a spark for transformation. Your unique voice and perspective have the potential to ripple outward, creating waves of innovation and connection. Leadership often begins with the simplest acts: extending kindness in a challenging moment, offering an idea that sparks discussion, or being an attentive listener when it matters most. These small actions knit together the fabric of collaboration and trust that fuels progress and cultivates pride in shared success.

Take a moment to internalize this truth: the ability to lead resides within you. Your authenticity and individuality are the very traits that inspire others to believe in their potential. Leadership is contagious. When you act with confidence and clarity, you encourage others to rise to their best selves. If that sense of potential feels distant right now, know it's waiting for you to tap into it. Together, we'll explore strategies to uncover your innate strengths and channel them into transformative leadership.

Leadership begins with self-awareness and the understanding that your unique qualities are assets in any setting. When you identify your strengths and learn to connect them to broader goals, you enhance your ability to collaborate and lay the groundwork for inspiring others. Authentic leadership builds a culture of innovation, inclusivity, and mutual respect—qualities that drive collective success and create a lasting legacy.

> **Leadership begins with self-awareness and the understanding that your unique qualities are assets in any setting.**

History is rich with examples of individuals who led with impact long before holding formal titles. These leaders didn't wait for permission; they saw opportunities for change and acted on them. Every time you reflect on your values, take an intentional step toward growth, or share a vision that brings others together because you embody the essence of leadership.

> **History is rich with examples of individuals who led with impact long before holding formal titles.**

Now is the time to amplify your influence. Regardless of your role, you can uplift, motivate, and create positive change. By stepping into this potential, you not only distinguish yourself but also lay the foundation for a future defined by purpose and achievement.

In the next section, we'll delve into actionable strategies to help you cultivate and demonstrate leadership in any situation. From forging meaningful connections to embracing adaptability and initiative, these principles will empower you to lead with confidence and authenticity.

Your perspective, energy, and ideas matter more than ever. Let's begin this transformative journey to elevate your leadership skills, broaden your impact, and set the stage for a brighter, more connected future. Your journey starts here—let's unlock the extraordinary leader within you!

REFLECTION: UNEARTHING YOUR LEADERSHIP POTENTIAL WITHOUT A TITLE

Before diving into strategies for leading without formal authority, take a moment to reflect on the profound influence you already possess. Leadership isn't about positions or hierarchies—it's about the impact you create in every interaction and the inspiration you bring to those around you. This reflection is your chance to recognize that leadership is within your reach, shaped not by titles but by intention, authenticity, and action.

The most transformative leaders often begin by understanding their unique ability to uplift others, spark ideas, and drive progress. These reflections are not just about self-awareness— they're about tuning into the possibilities you hold to shape your workplace, relationships, and personal growth. Reflecting on your strengths, challenges, and opportunities aligns you with impactful leadership.

Here are three thought-provoking questions to guide you in exploring your leadership potential:

1. **When have you inspired or influenced someone without holding a formal leadership role?** Reflect on when your words, actions, or ideas made a difference to someone or to your team. What did this experience teach you about your ability to lead by example and foster meaningful change?

2. **What unique strengths and perspectives do you bring to your workplace or community?** Consider the qualities, skills, or insights that set you apart. How do these attributes empower you to create value and inspire others, even without an official title?

3. **What opportunities exist in your current role to lead through action?** Think about challenges, gaps, or areas for improvement in your environment. How can you offer solutions, drive collaboration, or motivate your peers to work toward a shared goal?

Use these questions as a starting point to uncover the leader within you. Reflection isn't just about looking inward—it's about recognizing the profound ways you can shape the world around you. Leadership is less about authority and more about connection, influence, and the courage to act with purpose. Embrace this moment as your opportunity to ignite the change you wish to see and step into your power.

IGNITE YOUR CAREER PATH:
FIVE FUNDAMENTALS FOR EVERYDAY LEADERSHIP

In today's dynamic work environment, mastering these five key principles will help you unlock your leadership potential and drive both personal and professional growth.

Fundamental One. Unleash Your Potential: Shining Your Light as a Leader

Here's a truth I know: because you've chosen to explore leadership, you already possess the ability to shine brighter than most! Your ability to uplift others through empathy, attentiveness, and solution-focused thinking sets a powerful example. Now is the perfect moment to embrace that potential and allow your unique leadership style to illuminate not only your path but also the journeys of those around you.

> **Here's a truth I know: because you've chosen to explore leadership, you already possess the ability to shine brighter than most!**

Shining begins with bringing genuine enthusiasm and care to every task and interaction. When you approach challenges with optimism and determination, you create a ripple effect that raises the energy and focus of your team. Your attitude becomes an inspiration, encouraging those around you to adopt a similar commitment to excellence. This is the essence of human pride—a dynamic force that fuels creativity, collaboration, and enduring success in any environment.

> **This is the essence of human pride—a dynamic force that fuels creativity, collaboration, and enduring success in any environment.**

Here's the transformative insight: seize opportunities to uplift and support others. Look for colleagues who are striving to excel or navigating difficulties and make it a point to acknowledge their efforts. Imagine saying during a meeting, "Your presentation today was fantastic—it highlighted exactly what we needed. Let's collaborate more on similar projects." These small but meaningful gestures build confidence and foster an atmosphere where everyone feels empowered to contribute their best.

Another key to unlocking your leadership potential lies in practicing curiosity and active listening. In group discussions, make sure you hear every voice and actively seek diverse perspectives. A simple phrase like "I'd love to hear your take on this—you always bring fresh insights" can encourage others to share their ideas. This inclusive approach fosters respect, strengthens connections, and cultivates an innovative, forward-thinking workplace.

To magnify your influence, prioritize constructive feedback as a fundamental element of your leadership. Regularly invite input on your work while offering thoughtful feedback to others. Create opportunities for open dialogue by initiating feedback sessions or celebrating team milestones. For instance, host discussions where peers can share ideas for improvement and recognize achievements. These moments build trust, mutual growth, and a shared commitment to collective success.

Your potential is a powerful source of pride and the possibility that uplifts everyone it touches. By contributing positively, you inspire those around you to aim higher and work smarter. Your energy can spark a cultural shift that motivates others to embrace their own strengths and align with a shared vision of success.

Your potential is a powerful source of pride and the possibility that uplifts everyone it touches.

Take a moment to embrace this opportunity with confidence and purpose. This is your time to ignite enthusiasm, drive meaningful results, and create a workplace environment where pride and achievement flourish. Let your light shine—the impact of your leadership will ripple outward, leaving a legacy of growth and connection for yourself and those you inspire.

Fundamental Two. The Power of Influence: Leading with Impact Beyond Titles

Leading without a formal title is like being the **spark** that ignites dry kindling—your actions have the potential to fuel excitement, creativity, and motivation. Imagine starting each day knowing you can shape your workplace atmosphere through positivity and enthusiasm. By embracing challenges with a solution-oriented mindset, you inspire others to adopt the same energy and approach. Titles or hierarchies do not confine leadership; it's expressed in the small, consistent actions that build trust, foster collaboration, and evoke pride within your team.

As someone engaged in this book, you already recognize your unique potential to make a difference. Your everyday actions—whether sharing an innovative idea, offering a helping hand, or being a source of encouragement—create a ripple effect that transforms your surroundings. Think back to a time when you supported a colleague who was under pressure. Your encouragement eased their stress, strengthened your connection, and reinforced a culture of camaraderie. This ability to inspire through kindness, collaboration, and ingenuity lies at the heart of human pride, fueling innovation and resilience on both individual and collective levels.

Bringing enthusiasm and creativity to your work sets the stage for a dynamic, solution-focused environment. My retail career taught me the profound impact of taking initiative, whether managing individual stores or driving corporate-level transformations. Observing challenges on the front lines revealed unmet needs and opportunities for improvement, insights that informed meaningful changes. Your firsthand experiences offer unique perspectives on potential improvements. When you share constructive feedback and act on these insights, you not only influence your workplace, but you also inspire others to see themselves as catalysts for progress.

Consider stepping into your leadership potential by initiating informal brainstorming sessions or launching small pilot projects. For example, you could host a monthly "Idea Jam" where team members gather to propose minor changes that enhance processes or outcomes. Such gatherings spark creativity, invite diverse perspectives, and foster inclusivity. Similarly, taking the lead on a pilot project—perhaps streamlining a process or testing a new approach—demonstrates your ability to identify opportunities, think cleverly, and drive positive change. These initiatives reflect leadership in action, showcasing your commitment to shared goals and the success of your team.

In today's workplaces, rigid hierarchies are giving way to models built on shared ownership and collaboration. This shift creates space for everyone to lead, regardless of formal roles. Your ability to champion diverse ideas, celebrate others' contributions, and prioritize both personal and collective growth has never been more valuable. By stepping into this evolving definition of leadership, you contribute to workplaces where ingenuity, purpose, and potential flourish.

When we embrace influence beyond titles, we don't just achieve impressive results— we cultivate environments where pride in contribution drives continuous innovation.

When we embrace influence beyond titles, we don't just achieve impressive results— we cultivate environments where pride in contribution drives continuous innovation. Through these efforts, we transform workplaces into vibrant communities of shared ambition, creativity, and success. Together, we can build a future that reflects the best of human capability, proving that leadership is not about position but about impact.

Fundamental Three. Catalyst for Change: Transforming Ideas into Action

Inspiring change is more than just presenting compelling ideas— it's about **transforming** those ideas into reality. True leadership begins with inclusivity, embracing diverse perspectives, celebrating differences, and cultivating openness in every interaction. When you model these values, you create an environment where others feel empowered to express themselves and take pride in their unique contributions. This ripple effect establishes a workplace culture that values and amplifies every voice, building the foundation for collective success.

Collaboration and open communication are essential for turning ideas into actionable solutions. Creating regular opportunities for dialogue—whether through brainstorming sessions, team forums, or digital collaboration platforms—fosters a sense of belonging and shared purpose. For instance, consider hosting a monthly "Innovation Roundtable" where team members gather to share ideas, discuss challenges, and explore potential solutions. These sessions not only build trust but also remind everyone of their role in the bigger picture. Seeing their contributions drive progress inspires colleagues to engage more deeply, fueling both individual and team pride.

The real transformation begins when ideas move from discussion to execution. By addressing everyday challenges, such as

> **The real transformation begins when ideas move from discussion to execution.**

streamlining workflows, improving customer interactions, or enhancing internal communication, you show that leadership is rooted in action. These deliberate, solution-focused steps demonstrate your commitment to progress and inspire others to share their ideas. Leadership without a formal title shows the courage to make things better and the willingness to take meaningful action, no matter the scale of the challenge.

Imagine the fulfillment you'll experience when your efforts produce tangible results. By making a measurable impact, it affirms your leadership and fuels your motivation to keep pushing for progress. It also inspires others to follow your example, fostering a workplace culture where innovation becomes the norm. As your actions create visible improvements, you set a standard of excellence and create a ripple effect that encourages others to think creatively and act decisively.

Your ability to lead by example transforms challenges into opportunities. For instance, improving a process or solving a persistent problem can lead to increased efficiency, enhanced team morale, or even new business opportunities. These visible wins not only reinforce your value to the company but also cultivate a culture where everyone feels empowered to contribute. Every step forward builds momentum, proving that progress is a shared effort fueled by collaboration, creativity, and determination.

This is your moment to step into your leadership potential and inspire meaningful change. By embracing your creativity, determination, and proactive spirit, you pave the way for growth and success that benefits your entire workplace. Your actions show that leadership isn't confined to titles but is found in the courage to lead with purpose and conviction. Together, through your vision and commitment, you can unlock new possibilities and redefine what progress looks like for your team and company.

By embracing your creativity, determination, and proactive spirit, you pave the way for growth and success that benefits your entire workplace.

Fundamental Four. United We Succeed: Harnessing the Strength of Teamwork

The transformative power of collaboration lies in its simplicity: when people unite their perspectives, they create solutions far more innovative and impactful than any individual effort. **Teamwork** fosters a shared purpose and deep trust, connecting individual contributions to a collective mission. This connection ignites human pride, inspiring commitment, creativity, and a sense of belonging that transcends individual achievements.

To unlock the true potential of teamwork, cultivating an environment where everyone feels empowered to contribute is crucial. Simple yet powerful practices—like brainstorming sessions, roundtable discussions, or impromptu huddles—can spark exceptional ideas. Encourage team members to think boldly and embrace unconventional suggestions. After all, the most groundbreaking innovations often emerge from the boldest concepts. By ensuring everyone is heard and valued, you create a culture of confidence and collaboration where innovation flourishes.

Teamwork's strength lies not just within individual teams but across departments and disciplines. Cross-functional collaboration blends diverse expertise, generating holistic solutions that address complex challenges. Imagine a project where marketing, operations, and customer service collaborate to tackle customer feedback. Together, they can craft strategies that go beyond isolated fixes, enhancing communication, experience, and service delivery. This synergy showcases how shared efforts amplify outcomes, reinforcing the power of a united mission.

> **Leading in a collaborative environment is less about authority and more about creating space for others to excel.**

Leading in a collaborative environment is less about authority and more about creating space for others to excel. By championing inclusivity and fostering open communication, you set the tone for a workplace where mutual respect and shared responsibility thrive. This leadership by example ripples across teams, encouraging everyone to embrace collective efforts and shared successes. The outcome is not just stronger teams but a more cohesive workforce driven by trust and unity.

Visualize a workplace where collaboration fuels daily progress and innovation. Challenges are no longer obstacles but opportunities for collective problem-solving. The combined strengths of diverse perspectives transform goals into reality, and remarkable achievements become routine. In this environment, teamwork isn't just a strategy—it's a culture that drives lasting success.

As you embrace and champion collaboration, you inspire those around you to join in this vision. Together, unified efforts pave the way for brighter futures, greater opportunities, and workplaces that thrive on shared potential. Step boldly into your role as a catalyst for teamwork and witness the extraordinary power of unity unfold. Your leadership can shape a culture where collaboration is the foundation for every success.

Fundamental Five. Learning Together: Building a Knowledge-Driven Workplace

Knowledge forms the cornerstone of meaningful progress, and you have the power to nurture an environment where learning and growth flourish. A workplace driven by knowledge doesn't just enhance individual skills—it energizes the entire company, fostering a dynamic atmosphere of innovation, collaboration, and shared success. By prioritizing continuous learning, you unlock your potential and the brilliance of those around you, creating pride and purpose that resonates throughout the team.

Establishing a culture of knowledge begins with curiosity and open dialogue. Encourage colleagues to ask thoughtful questions, explore uncharted ideas, and share their insights openly. When people feel

> **Establishing a culture of knowledge begins with curiosity and open dialogue.**

empowered to contribute their perspectives, engagement and innovation naturally follow. Opportunities such as interactive workshops, team learning sessions, and professional development resources are essential in creating an environment where knowledge flows seamlessly. These initiatives do more than sharpen individual skills. They foster connection, teamwork, and a collective sense of achievement.

Start small with accessible initiatives that inspire excitement about learning. For instance, suggest hosting "Lunch and Learn" sessions where team members present topics they are passionate about or share expertise in areas of interest. Imagine your colleagues gathering to explore industry trends, innovative tools, and unique approaches to problem-solving. These sessions deepen understanding and build camaraderie and a sense of shared purpose. A weekly spotlight during team meetings on a new skill, tool, or best practice can set the tone for a ripple effect of curiosity and collaboration.

Collaborative learning amplifies impact. Establish a shared library of resources—digital articles, tutorials, or e-books—where team members can contribute and benefit equally. You might also consider cross-departmental initiatives like job-shadowing or project exchanges, where employees gain fresh perspectives and forge stronger connections. Such efforts underline the value of diverse expertise, cultivating a culture where learning from one another is both encouraged and celebrated.

Your involvement in these learning initiatives shows your commitment to excellence and growth. Lead by example: share books, podcasts, or articles that have inspired you, or propose a discussion around a trending topic in your industry. Get together with others to learn about new technologies and the best ways to use them. These actions show your dedication to personal and professional development, inspiring your peers to join you on this journey and amplifying the collective momentum toward growth.

Now, imagine the impact of a workplace where we weave the pursuit of knowledge into its very fabric. Team members, energized by the opportunity to learn and grow, take pride in their contributions, fueling both individual and collective success. This shared commitment to learning drives creativity, strengthens collaboration, and sets the stage for continuous innovation.

By promoting a culture of learning, you create an environment of trust, unity, and excellence. Your leadership not only enhances skills but also builds stronger bonds and propels your workplace toward industry leadership. As curiosity becomes the standard and knowledge-sharing becomes second nature, you'll witness transformations in morale, creativity, and overall performance.

Take the lead today in cultivating a workplace where learning thrives. Celebrate curiosity, foster collaboration, and inspire pride in collective growth. Together, you and your colleagues will unlock additional levels of potential and achievement, building a brighter and more innovative future for all.

As curiosity becomes the standard and knowledge-sharing becomes second nature, you'll witness transformations in morale, creativity, and overall performance.

ESSENTIAL TAKEAWAYS
FOR LEADERSHIP WITHOUT TITLES

Leadership is often associated with titles, but true influence stems from your actions and values.

Leadership Through Influence

True leadership transcends titles and roles. It's not about authority but about the actions you take to shape your environment and inspire those around you. Leadership through influence begins with empathy, collaboration, and a solution-oriented mindset. When you show these qualities consistently, you create a ripple effect that fosters pride, trust, and innovation.

Your ability to lead without a title comes from the respect you earn through your actions, especially when they align with shared values. This respect becomes the foundation of your influence, inspiring others to follow your example. By being consistent and authentic, you prove that leadership is about impact, not position, and show that genuine leaders are defined by the way they inspire, uplift, and drive progress.

Acting as a Catalyst for Progress

Great leaders look for ways to improve things and make their ideas a reality. You don't need a formal title to bring about meaningful change. You foster an inclusive environment where diverse perspectives are celebrated and explored and leadership emerges. In such a space, collaboration becomes the engine that drives progress, allowing challenges to be tackled creatively and as a team.

Taking initiative—whether by piloting a project, proposing an idea, or facilitating a critical conversation—demonstrates that leadership is about stepping forward with conviction. Your courage to lead by example shows that progress is not a one-person job but the result of unified efforts. By catalyzing action, you inspire those around you to see opportunities instead of obstacles, driving innovation and creating a lasting impact.

Building Collaboration as the Foundation for Success

Teamwork amplifies potential, creating outcomes that far exceed what individuals can achieve on their own. Leadership within a team is not about giving orders; it's about facilitating collaboration. By fostering open communication, championing inclusivity, and encouraging every voice to be heard, you create an environment where people feel valued and empowered to share their best ideas.

This approach builds unity, strengthens trust, and fuels innovation. When everyone feels ownership of the team's success, shared ambition becomes a powerful motivator. As a collaborative leader, you focus on creating a culture where cooperation, creativity, and shared responsibility thrive. In such an environment, the team achieves success through collective effort, with every member contributing to the outcome.

Learning as a Leadership Tool

Knowledge is power, and fostering a culture of learning is one of the most impactful ways to show leadership. By promoting curiosity, sharing resources, and creating development opportunities, you build an environment where growth is a shared pursuit.

Leading through learning starts with modeling curiosity—whether by embracing feedback, sharing insights, or seeking opportunities to improve. When you prioritize growth, you encourage others to adopt the same mindset, fostering a workplace culture that thrives on continuous improvement.

This foundation of learning fosters pride in both individual and collective accomplishments, driving teams toward greater innovation and success. It reinforces the idea that every new skill, insight, or experience contributes to a shared vision of excellence.

Authenticity as Your Leadership Anchor

Your greatest leadership tool is your authenticity. By embracing your unique qualities and strengths, you create a powerful ripple effect that inspires others to do the same. Authentic leadership fosters trust, encourages openness, and builds a culture where people feel safe to express ideas, take risks, and contribute fully.

When you lead with integrity and vulnerability, you set a standard that empowers others to follow suit. By showing up as your true self, you give permission for others to embrace their authenticity, too.

This fosters deeper connections and a shared sense of purpose, encouraging teams to collaborate more meaningfully and work toward shared goals with enthusiasm and confidence.

Unlocking Potential Through Everyday Leadership

These five fundamentals—influence, initiative, collaboration, learning, and authenticity—highlight that leadership is accessible to everyone who acts with intention, empathy, and courage. You don't need a title to inspire change, drive innovation, or create meaningful connections.

These principles foster a workplace culture that celebrates shared success, valued contributions, and collective progress. Leadership without titles is not only possible—it's transformative.

Step into your potential. Lead with authenticity. Start creating your impact today.

YOUR NEXT STEPS: LEADING THROUGH ACTION AND AUTHENTICITY

Formal roles or titles do not confine leadership—your ability to inspire, influence, and drive change from wherever you stand defines it. By embracing your unique strengths and committing to fostering collaboration and growth, you can create a lasting impact on your workplace and beyond.

1. Recognize Your Inner Leader

Leadership starts from within.

- ▶ Embrace your power to influence and inspire others.

- Acknowledge your unique strengths and how they contribute to the bigger picture.

Action Step: Reflect on a recent moment where your actions positively impacted a colleague or team. Identify what made this moment successful and how you can replicate it in the future.

2. Lead by Example

Demonstrate leadership through action, not authority

- Be proactive in offering solutions, supporting others, and sharing your ideas.
- Model the behaviors you want to see, fostering a culture of trust and collaboration.

Action Step: Identify one slight change where you can lead in your workplace, such as streamlining a process or organizing a team discussion. Bring this idea to life.

3. Empower Those Around You

Great leaders uplift others.

- Acknowledge and celebrate your colleagues' efforts and contributions.
- Foster an inclusive environment where everyone feels valued and heard.

Action Step: This week, recognize a colleague's specific achievement or effort. Offer encouragement to reinforce their value to the team.

4. Cultivate Collaboration

Harness the power of teamwork to drive innovation.

- ▶ Encourage open communication and diverse perspectives.
- ▶ Create opportunities for group problem-solving and shared success.

Action Step: Organize a brainstorming session or collaborative meeting to address a current challenge. Invite input from colleagues in various departments and backgrounds.

5. Commit to Continuous Growth

Champion a culture of learning and curiosity.

- ▶ Encourage knowledge-sharing and provide access to learning resources.
- ▶ Celebrate personal and team development milestones.

Action Step: Propose a "Lunch and Learn" session or start a shared resource library in your workplace. Lead by sharing an article, podcast, or book that has inspired you.

Your Leadership Legacy

Leadership is a journey of continuous growth and intentional action. By recognizing your ability to influence and inspire, you set the foundation for a workplace where everyone can thrive. Whether through small gestures or significant initiatives, your commitment to uplifting others creates a ripple effect of pride, innovation, and shared success.

Step into your power as a leader without a title and watch as your actions inspire a culture of collaboration, curiosity, and excellence. Together, you and your team can achieve remarkable outcomes that reflect the best of human potential.

PART 3

FOR YOURSELF

Personal Evolution Through Human Potential

These five pillars—journaling, mindfulness, gratitude, meditation, and flow—are not just tools; they're invitations to engage more deeply with your life.

CHAPTER 9

CELEBRATING YOUR UNIQUE HUMANITY

Harnessing Your Strengths for Unstoppable Success

Take a deep breath. This moment is yours. Reaching the final chapter is more than just finishing a book—it's a bold declaration of your commitment to growth, courage, and potential. This isn't the end of the journey; it's a powerful beginning, inviting you to embrace your unique humanity and the incredible impact only you can make.

EMBRACING WHAT TRULY MATTERS

On my fifty-fifth birthday in May 2019, life delivered an unexpected wake-up call. A medical diagnosis shattered my illusion of invincibility, forcing me to reevaluate my priorities. After six more years and another health challenge, I discovered a universal truth: life's value isn't found in accolades or possessions but in the love we give, the connections we build, and the authenticity we live by.

These experiences have transformed me. They softened my resilience, replacing it with patience, grace, and empathy. They

> **Through life's trials, I've discovered the transformative power of intentional living, turning even the most difficult moments into opportunities for growth and connection.**

taught me that vulnerability isn't a weakness—it's a superpower, creating authentic relationships and fostering deeper understanding. Through life's trials, I've discovered the transformative power of intentional living, turning even the most difficult moments into opportunities for growth and connection.

A JOURNEY OF TRANSFORMATION

The summer of 2019 brought another pivotal moment: a men's retreat in upstate New York. For three days, I joined seventy-five strangers in an emotional experience of storytelling, reflection, and raw vulnerability. One moment, in particular, stands out—a powerful "anger ceremony" that called us to confront and release deeply buried emotions. Amid tears and primal screams, I realized true strength lies in feeling deeply and connecting openly.

Returning home, I felt transformed. My relationships became more intentional, rooted in honesty, respect, and purpose. This shift in perspective inspired another bold step: selling nearly everything my husband and I owned, buying an Airstream, and embarking on a fourteen-month journey we called the "Retail in America Tour."

That journey became so much more than an exploration of retail— it was a celebration of humanity. We listened to stories around campfires, witnessed sunsets that painted the sky, and marveled at the quiet resilience of nature. These moments reminded me of what truly matters: the simplicity of life, the depth of human connection, and the beauty of shared humanity.

THE POWER OF YOUR STORY

If there's one truth I've uncovered, it's this: your humanity is your greatest superpower. It's the unique combination of your strengths, values, and dreams that defines you. By embracing your individuality, you inspire others to do the same.

You don't need a title to lead. Leadership is authenticity—it's showing up with intention, living with purpose, and making a difference in the lives you touch.

> **If there's one truth I've uncovered, it's this: your humanity is your greatest superpower.**

Life's challenges have deepened my gratitude, strengthened my relationships, and taught me to lead with empathy. This is the essence of pride—recognizing your worth and living boldly in alignment with your values.

REFLECTION PROMPTS

Before we part ways, I invite you to reflect on your journey and the lessons it has revealed. Let these prompts guide you in celebrating your unique humanity:

1. **What makes you feel most alive?** Reflect on the moments when you've felt deeply connected or inspired. How can you create more of these experiences?
2. **How have challenges shaped you?** Think about the obstacles you've overcome and the strengths you've discovered. How can these insights inspire and uplift others?
3. **What legacy do you want to leave?** Envision the impact you want to have on the people and communities around you. What steps can you take today to align with that vision?

THE JOURNEY AHEAD

As you close this chapter, know this: you are just beginning. Within you lies a limitless capacity for growth, connection, and impact. Embrace your story, honor your values, and lead with pride.

The world is waiting for the light only you can shine. Step forward with confidence. Lead with love. Live with purpose. And remember: the most extraordinary journeys begin when you have the courage to celebrate the incredible person you already are.

Your journey starts now.

UNLOCK AUTHENTICITY AND STRENGTHS: FIVE PILLARS FOR PERSONAL GROWTH

These five pillars will guide you in unlocking your true authenticity and strength.

Pillar One. Inspire Personal Development: Techniques for Self-Discovery

Embarking on a journey of personal growth isn't just about improvement—it's about uncovering your essence and claiming your power. It's about **celebrating your humanity** and aligning with the life you're meant to live.

Establishing intentional practices like self-reflection, mindfulness, and gratitude doesn't just reshape your days—it transforms how you see yourself and the

> **Establishing intentional practices like self-reflection, mindfulness, and gratitude doesn't just reshape your days—it transforms how you see yourself and the world.**

world. Imagine waking up with a deep sense of clarity and purpose, feeling grounded and empowered to tackle whatever lies ahead. That clarity doesn't just inspire resilience—it unlocks the potential to create a life brimming with meaning and fulfillment.

Let's explore the transformative tools that have fueled my growth and can guide yours.

Journaling: A Mirror to Your Inner World

Journaling isn't just writing—it's a dialogue with your soul. It gives you a space to pour out thoughts, process emotions, and uncover the insights that illuminate your path.

Set aside time daily to jot down your reflections. You don't need to write a novel—just capture your emotions, celebrate minor victories, or reflect on challenges. Use prompts like:

- ▶ "What made me feel alive today?"
- ▶ "What am I proud of this week?"
- ▶ "What did a recent challenge teach me?"

Revisit your entries over time to uncover patterns and recognize the threads of your authentic self.

Mindfulness: Anchoring Yourself in the Present

In a noisy, fast-paced world, mindfulness is your anchor to the present moment. It's about observing your thoughts and emotions without judgment, helping you reconnect with your values and passions.

Start small. Take a few moments daily to focus on your breath or immerse yourself in simple activities, like enjoying a cup of tea.

These moments of presence help quiet the noise and tune into your inner truth.

Distractions, like endless scrolling and notifications, can steal this clarity. Stepping back can be profoundly liberating. While writing this book, I removed apps from my phone, freeing energy for creativity and self-reflection.

Gratitude: Cultivating a Heart Full of Joy

Gratitude shifts your focus from what's missing to what's abundant, which rewires your brain to notice life's beauty. It turns ordinary moments into sources of joy.

Start a gratitude journal and, each night, write three things you're thankful for—whether it's a heartfelt conversation, a brilliant sunrise, or the feeling of completing a task. Over time, this practice becomes a well of positivity, helping you navigate life's challenges.

Gratitude extends beyond writing—it's in the small acts: a heartfelt thank you, a smile of appreciation, or an acknowledgment of someone's kindness. These acts strengthen connections and remind us of life's interconnected beauty.

Meditation: Discovering Stillness amid Chaos

Meditation is your journey inward, creating space to breathe, observe, and reconnect with your core. It's not about silencing your mind but cultivating awareness and acceptance.

Begin with just five minutes of deep breathing or a guided session. Over time, meditation reveals patterns, provides clarity, and strengthens your ability to approach challenges with grace.

For me, meditation hasn't always been easy, but I've learned to embrace its imperfections. Each moment spent meditating—however brief—brings me closer to inner peace and self-understanding.

Creating Flow: The Art of Engagement

Flow is the magical state where time fades, and your energy aligns effortlessly with your passion. It's when you're so immersed in an activity, it feels like pure joy.

For me, writing this book became such a state—an act of creation free from distraction. Finding your flow begins with identifying activities that ignite your creativity and bring you joy—whether it's painting, cooking, gardening, or brainstorming new ideas.

Flow isn't just about hobbies; it's a pathway to fulfillment and growth.

Your Path to Authenticity Starts Here

These five pillars—**journaling, mindfulness, gratitude, meditation, and flow**—are not just tools; they're invitations to engage more deeply with your life. They remind you to honor your humanity, celebrate your progress, and embrace each step of your journey, even when the path feels uncertain.

These five pillars—journaling, mindfulness, gratitude, meditation, and flow—are not just tools; they're invitations to engage more deeply with your life.

Growth isn't linear. Some days will challenge you, but those moments are opportunities to realign with your purpose. Your imperfections are part of your beauty, and your humanity is your strength.

Now is your time to nurture your soul, ignite your potential, and let your authentic self shine brightly. The journey begins with one step: the choice to say yes to yourself.

Welcome the adventure. Celebrate every milestone and know that each moment brings you closer to becoming the fullest version of you.

Step forward with courage and let your brilliance shine.

Pillar Two. Unlock Your Potential: The Journey of Continuous Learning

Learning something new is one of the most profound ways to embrace your humanity and celebrate your limitless potential. Each skill you explore and each subject you dive into is an invitation to uncover hidden layers of your authentic self. Through these explorations, you'll reignite dormant passions and gain clarity about what matters in your life.

Learning isn't just about gaining knowledge—it's about transformation. It challenges you to step beyond your comfort zone, expand your adaptability, and open your mind to new possibilities.

My journey began in a setting like this— a men's retreat where storytelling and vulnerability revealed truths I hadn't dared to face.

Whether through a class, workshop, or group activity, these experiences connect you with like-minded individuals, enriching your perspective through shared stories and mutual discovery. My journey began in a setting like this—a men's retreat where storytelling and vulnerability revealed truths I hadn't dared to face.

Are You Ready to Step into the Unknown?

Embarking on the adventure of learning isn't just a change of pace—it's an act of courage. It's a decision to embrace uncertainty and uncover parts of yourself you've yet to meet. When you dare to leave the familiar behind, you often stumble upon the most fulfilling experiences—ones that reveal your true potential and infuse your life with purpose.

The Power of Exploration

Leaping into learning—whether mastering a new hobby, diving into a different field, or pursuing personal growth—activates your natural curiosity. This curiosity sparks creativity and invites fresh perspectives into your life. Exploration isn't about perfection or expertise; it's about the joy of discovery.

Imagine trying something completely new—painting, writing poetry, or strumming a guitar for the first time. The act becomes the reward, free from expectations or deadlines. I still remember picking up a guitar after watching *A Star Is Born*. While I didn't stick with it for long, those months brought me a sense of creativity and fulfillment I hadn't felt in years.

Every new interest, whether fleeting or enduring, deepens the connection to your authentic self. It reveals what excites you, what challenges you, and what resonates most deeply within your spirit. From experimenting with gourmet cooking to capturing stunning photographs, every pursuit is an opportunity to express your uniqueness.

The Thrill of Discovery

There's a unique exhilaration in stepping into the unknown. Imagine the thrill of trying goat yoga, taking a pottery class, or learning a new sport. These moments aren't just about acquiring skills— they're about rediscovering yourself.

Even if a hobby doesn't become a permanent part of your life, it leaves a lasting mark. Each attempt teaches you something new about your motivations, your joy, and how to tap into your potential. For me, returning to the guitar is on the horizon—not because I need to master it but because of the introspection and joy it brought me.

Nurturing Creativity and Building Community

Exploring new interests often leads to more than personal growth— it becomes a bridge to connecting with others. Shared passions create vibrant communities where ideas and inspiration surge.

Picture the sense of belonging that comes from engaging with a group that shares your excitement. These connections foster camaraderie and empowerment as you inspire and support one another's growth.

The skills you develop—whether technical or creative—enhance your confidence and remind you that you are capable of change, growth, and innovation.

Answering the Call to Adventure

Take that leap. Step outside the comfortable rhythm of your daily life and embrace the adventure of learning something new. Each step, no matter how small, unveils a version of yourself waiting to be celebrated.

This is your invitation to ignite your curiosity, explore the unknown, and uncover a richer, more dynamic version

> **Continuous learning isn't just about acquiring skills—it's about discovering who you are and embracing the infinite possibilities of your unique humanity.**

of yourself. Continuous learning isn't just about acquiring skills—it's about discovering who you are and embracing the infinite possibilities of your unique humanity.

Let this be the moment you say yes to exploration. Let it be the moment you realize learning is not just an activity but a celebration of your potential and a pathway to becoming your truest self.

Your journey begins now. Move forward with curiosity and courage, and watch your potential unfold.

Pillar Three. Embrace Your Strengths: The Path to Self-Awareness and Authenticity

Have you ever felt stuck in the endless loop of setting goals that focus on fixing your weaknesses? Those unfulfilled New Year's resolutions, the heavy "shoulds" that seem to define progress, or the dreaded question in interviews: "What are your weaknesses?" I know I've been there.

> **A strength-based approach amplifies your talents and sparks personal and professional growth.**

It's time to rewrite that narrative. Instead of dwelling on what needs improvement, shift your focus to **what makes you powerful**. A strength-based approach amplifies your talents and sparks personal and professional growth. By celebrating your unique contributions, you boost your confidence, inspire others, and create a ripple effect that encourages those around you to embrace their strengths, too.

The Power of Strength-Based Growth

Focusing on your strengths transforms how you approach challenges. It fosters collaboration and innovation by encouraging diverse talents to shine, making problem-solving more creative and achievements more fulfilling. In a strength-driven environment, resilience thrives, and progress feels exciting—not forced. This mindset values individuality, turning it into a collective advantage that drives success.

Your unique talents and potential set you apart in today's competitive world.

Reflecting on Your Strengths

Take a moment to think about what comes naturally to you. Recall times when you've felt proud of your work or received compliments that truly resonated. What were you doing in those moments? Were you connecting with others, solving problems, or creating something new? Those moments hold the key to recognizing the abilities that make you exceptional.

> **Everything changed when I embraced self-reflection and stopped measuring myself against others' benchmarks.**

For years, I struggled with self-acceptance. I was constantly chasing an ideal—trying to be better, faster, more present. That relentless pursuit, fueled by comparisons and external pressures, left me drained and unfulfilled. Everything changed when I embraced self-reflection and stopped measuring myself against others' benchmarks. I recognized my value, appreciated my achievements, and set authentic goals aligned with my pace and priorities.

The Shift to Self-Acceptance

Self-acceptance isn't about striving for perfection; it's about honoring what makes you uniquely you. Ask honest questions like:

- ▶ "What am I truly good at?"
- ▶ "How can my strengths benefit others?"

I moved from stressing over shortcomings to focusing on my natural talents. This shift freed me to channel my energy into areas where I could truly excel. It boosted my confidence, enriched my relationships, and opened doors to opportunities that aligned with my purpose.

Harnessing Strengths in Your Career

Adopting a strength-based mindset redefines how you approach opportunities. Whether it's an interview or networking, leading with your strengths positions you as confident and authentic. Articulating your values and skills draws roles that align with your aspirations, making the job market feel less intimidating and more like a journey of self-discovery.

When you align your career with your strengths, the work you do feels meaningful and rewarding. You're no longer trying to fit into molds that don't suit you—you're creating a path that celebrates what makes you exceptional.

When you align your career with your strengths, the work you do feels meaningful and rewarding.

A Challenge to Embrace Your Strengths

Big ideas? Maybe. But here's the challenge: invest in your strengths. Reflect on your abilities, practice self-awareness, and trust that what makes you unique will lead to opportunities that feel authentic and fulfilling.

Your strengths are your greatest assets. By nurturing them, you'll create a life that celebrates who you truly are and paves a path that's meaningful and rewarding.

Start now—take that first step toward self-awareness and watch as your potential unfolds in ways you never imagined.

You are powerful just as you are. Embrace it. Celebrate it. And let your strengths lead the way.

Pillar Four. Creating Ripple Effects: Celebrating Human Potential Through Community Engagement

Imagine a world where even the smallest actions spark positive change—not just for you but for everyone around you. Engaging in volunteer work that aligns with your values transforms this vision into reality. **Dedicating your time**, **skills**, and **energy** to causes you care about isn't just an act of kindness—it's a chance to uplift others while fostering a profound sense of pride and purpose within yourself.

The Connection Between Service and Pride

When you share your unique talents through service—whether mentoring, taking part in environmental initiatives, or helping at a local shelter—you amplify your positive impact. Every effort, no matter how small, builds meaningful connections and enhances your sense of purpose. Beyond benefiting others, these actions also strengthen your identity within your community, reminding you of the incredible potential we all hold to create change.

Reflecting on my journey, I found immense joy in aligning my skills with causes that matter deeply to me. Many people wish to give back but are unsure how to start. Turning hesitation into action is the first step toward a ripple effect of growth, connection, and transformation.

Reflecting on my journey, I found immense joy in aligning my skills with causes that matter deeply to me.

My Journey: Turning Professional Expertise Into Impact

In January 2018, as a vice president of retail for a large company, I found myself with new opportunities to give back. I had aspired to serve on a nonprofit board and finally asked myself:

- ▶ "What are my strengths?"
- ▶ "Where can I make a real difference?"

The answer was clear: Goodwill.

After months of thoughtful discussion, I joined the Board of Directors for Goodwill New York/New Jersey, an organization with a century-long legacy of empowering individuals with disabilities and barriers to employment. This role became even more critical during the COVID-19 pandemic. While managing my responsibilities in my current role, I supported Goodwill's leadership through the crisis in the heart of NYC.

Instead of financial contributions, I offered my expertise in retail operations and training, helping reopen stores across multiple states. These stores not only provided jobs but also served as critical donation centers during a time of immense need. The pride I felt knowing my skills could create value during such a pivotal moment remains one of the most rewarding chapters of my professional life.

Harnessing Your Unique Strengths

Each of us has unique talents that can make a profound difference in our communities. By reflecting on your skills and asking where you can have the most impact, you can take meaningful steps toward transforming lives.

Consider:

- ▶ What are you passionate about?
- ▶ What strengths can you share?
- ▶ Which causes align with your values?

Even small contributions—like mentoring a student, supporting a food drive, or joining a community initiative—create ripples of change. These actions foster progress and positivity, not just for those you help but also for yourself, enhancing your sense of fulfillment and pride.

Building a Legacy of Positivity

When we embrace the power of community engagement, we don't just help individuals; we create lasting legacies. By sharing your gifts, you inspire others to do the same, building a culture of contribution and collaboration that strengthens communities and changes lives.

This is how we amplify human potential:

- By **uplifting others**, we grow as individuals.
- By **celebrating strengths**, we foster resilience and innovation.
- By **taking action**, we inspire those around us to do the same.

Your Invitation to Make an Impact

Now is your moment to step forward. Share your unique talents, take action that aligns with your passions, and witness the incredible ripple effect your efforts can create. When you embrace the power of contribution, you not only uplift others but deepen your sense of purpose, pride, and fulfillment.

What you do makes a difference. Together, we can build a brighter future—one that celebrates human potential strengthens communities, and leaves a legacy of hope and inspiration.

Take that first step. The world is waiting for your light.

Take that first step. The world is waiting for your light.

Pillar Five. Elevate Your Potential: The Triad of Health, Nutrition, and Rest

Here's a truth we often overlook when life gets overwhelming: your full potential depends on your commitment to **physical activity, nutrition**, and **rest**. These aren't abstract concepts—they are the pillars of vitality and resilience. I've learned this not just from years of experience but through my health challenges, which underscored how critical these habits are for maintaining a vibrant, purpose-driven life.

By embracing these essentials, I've rediscovered the energy to flourish and continue building a fulfilling, impactful existence. Now, it's your turn.

The Transformative Power of Physical Activity

Consistent movement does more than strengthen your body— it sharpens your mind and prepares you to face life's challenges with clarity and confidence. The rush of endorphins from exercise elevates your mood, enhances focus, and creates a sense of accomplishment that ripples into every area of your life.

And here's the best part: you don't need expensive equipment or a complex plan—just the commitment to show up for yourself. A brisk walk, a yoga session, or a few minutes of stretching can be enough to set transformation in motion.

Nutrition: Fueling Your Vitality

What you feed your body has a direct impact on your energy, emotions, and ability to achieve your goals. Nourishing yourself with wholesome, nutrient-rich foods doesn't just sustain your physical health—it supports mental clarity and emotional well-being.

Every mindful choice at the table is an investment in your future, enabling you to approach your ambitions and relationships with vitality and resilience. When you prioritize nutrition, you're choosing a life where energy and strength flourish, propelling you toward your best self.

The Underrated Power of Rest

Sleep is the cornerstone of restoration. It's when your body heals, your mind processes experiences, and creativity finds its footing. Without quality rest, even the best efforts in exercise and nutrition can falter.

Rest isn't a luxury—it's a nonnegotiable necessity. By prioritizing consistent, restorative sleep, you prepare yourself to greet each day with clarity and enthusiasm, ready to embrace opportunities and overcome challenges.

The Symphony of Balance

Together, physical activity, mindful eating, and restful sleep form a symphony of well-being. This triad creates the foundation for a thriving life, elevating your physical health, sharpening your mind, and fortifying your emotional resilience. When nurtured in harmony, these habits allow you to excel, bringing your best self to every endeavor.

My Journey: A Testament to Vitality

As I've entered my sixties, I've celebrated the vitality these mindful choices have cultivated. Even in the face of uncertainty, I've found strength and purpose by prioritizing movement, nourishment, and rest. Each day feels like a renewed opportunity to embrace the vibrant life I've created.

Your Potential Awaits

Your potential is waiting for you to unlock it. Take the first step today: lace up your running shoes, prepare a nutrient-rich meal, or set a consistent bedtime. These small, deliberate actions are the building blocks of a more empowered, fulfilling future.

Celebrate Your Journey

Rejoice in the vibrant tapestry of your life, knowing that every choice to nurture your well-being is paving the way for a healthier, stronger, and more confident version of yourself.

The journey begins now. Seize it, celebrate it, and elevate your life to heights you never thought possible.

ESSENTIAL TAKEAWAYS
FOR CELEBRATING YOUR HUMANITY

> **Celebrating your humanity involves recognizing and embracing the core elements that make you uniquely you.**

Celebrating your humanity involves recognizing and embracing the core elements that make you uniquely you. By reflecting on these essential takeaways, you can create a life that is not only authentic but also deeply fulfilling.

Define Your Core Values

Your core values are the compass guiding your decisions, relationships, and aspirations. They reflect what truly matters to you and provide a foundation for living an authentic, meaningful life.

Take time to reflect and answer these questions:

- ▶ What experiences bring you the greatest joy?
- ▶ What principles feel nonnegotiable?

Is it connection, creativity, or a sense of achievement? When your actions align with these values, life feels deeply fulfilling. Your values also empower you to set boundaries, prioritize commitments, and pursue opportunities that resonate with your true self.

Embrace Vulnerability as Strength

Vulnerability is not a weakness—it's a profound strength that fosters trust and connection. Sharing your true self, including your fears and hopes, inspires authenticity in your relationships and encourages others to do the same.

Imagine the courage it takes to admit when you don't have all the answers or to seek help. These moments of honesty build resilience and strengthen bonds, reminding us we're not alone in our challenges. Vulnerability opens the door to deeper understanding and growth for everyone involved.

Pursue Continuous Learning

Growth is a lifelong journey, not a destination. By staying curious and open to new experiences, you uncover talents, passions, and perspectives that enrich your life.

Step outside your comfort zone. Take a course, try a new hobby, or engage in thought-provoking conversations. Learning fosters adaptability and sparks creativity,

Growth is a lifelong journey, not a destination.

equipping you to navigate life's complexities. It's not just about acquiring knowledge but about evolving into the best version of yourself.

Leverage Your Unique Capabilities in Service

Your skills and strengths are powerful tools for creating a meaningful impact in your community. By offering your time, expertise, and kindness, you uplift others while cultivating a deep sense of pride and purpose.

Every act of service—no matter how small—creates a ripple effect of positivity. Mentoring someone, supporting local initiatives, or offering encouragement builds a legacy of progress and connection. By giving back, you enrich your own life and contribute to a more compassionate world.

Prioritize Your Well-Being

Your well-being is the foundation of everything else. Physical activity, mindful nutrition, and restorative sleep are not luxuries— they're essential for living a vibrant, fulfilling life.

> **Taking care of your body and mind equips you with the energy, focus, and resilience to pursue your goals and nurture relationships.**

Taking care of your body and mind equips you with the energy, focus, and resilience to pursue your goals and nurture relationships. These habits empower you to face challenges with confidence and seize opportunities with enthusiasm. Prioritizing your health is an investment in your potential and your future.

Embracing Your Unique Humanity

Defining your values, embracing vulnerability, pursuing learning, giving back, and prioritizing well-being—these principles form a roadmap to authenticity and fulfillment. They remind you that your humanity is your greatest strength, a wellspring of connection, growth, and inspiration.

As you integrate these practices into your life, remember: the journey is ongoing. Celebrate your progress, learn from your setbacks, and honor the qualities that make you uniquely you. By doing so, you'll not only enrich your own life but also inspire others to embrace their humanity, creating a world filled with compassion and possibility.

Step forward boldly. Celebrate your journey. Let your unique humanity shine.

Step forward boldly. Celebrate your journey. Let your unique humanity shine.

YOUR NEXT STEPS: HONORING YOUR UNIQUE PATH

Congratulations! You've reached the final chapter of this transformative journey. This isn't just the end of a book; it's the beginning of a new chapter in your life—one where you fully embrace your unique humanity, authentic strengths, and the limitless potential within you.

Take a moment to celebrate the effort you've put into your personal growth and self-discovery. You've done the work, and now it's time to apply these lessons to create a life that feels fulfilling, impactful, and unapologetically you.

1. Define Your Core Values

Your core values are your North Star, guiding every decision and aspiration. Clarity comes from understanding what matters most to you and aligning your life around these principles.

- ► Reflect on experiences that made you feel proud or fulfilled—what values were present in those moments?
- ► Ensure your personal and professional life aligns with these guiding principles.

Action Step: Take ten minutes to journal the values that resonate most with you. Identify when you felt deeply connected to your purpose and explore what values shaped that experience.

2. Embrace Vulnerability as a Strength

Vulnerability is your gateway to connection and growth. By sharing your authentic self, you build trust and strengthen relationships, fostering an environment of openness and empathy.

- ► Recognize vulnerability as a powerful tool that builds deeper bonds.
- ► Take small steps to share your true feelings or thoughts in conversations, projects, or relationships.

Action Step: Identify one area where you can practice vulnerability. Commit to sharing something authentic—whether it's a fear, a hope, or an idea—and notice how it deepens your connection with others.

3. Commit to Continuous Learning

Growth is a lifelong journey. Every new skill, hobby, or experience you pursue unlocks hidden talents and expands your perspective.

- ► Seek opportunities to try something outside your comfort zone, whether it's a workshop, hobby, or thought-provoking conversation.

- Embrace discomfort as part of the learning process—it's where growth happens.

Action Step: Sign up for an activity or class that excites and challenges you. Whether it's learning a language, exploring a new art form, or diving into a professional development course, take that leap toward exploration.

4. Leverage Your Strengths to Serve Others

Your unique talents hold the power to uplift and inspire. By aligning your skills with causes you care about, you create meaningful connections and contribute to a better world.

- Recognize the pride and fulfillment that comes from using your strengths to help others.
- Seek opportunities to mentor, volunteer, and support initiatives that align with your passions.

Action Step: Research a local volunteer opportunity or identify someone in your field you could mentor. Choose one way to use your strengths to give back this week.

5. Prioritize Your Well-Being

Your health is the foundation for everything else. When you prioritize your physical and mental well-being, you build the energy and resilience needed to pursue your goals.

- Commit to habits that enhance your body, mind, and spirit, such as exercise, mindful eating, and consistent rest.
- Recognize that self-care fuels your creativity and focus, enabling you to thrive.

Action Step: Choose one habit to focus on this week—whether it's a daily walk, cooking a healthy meal, or setting a consistent bedtime. Start small but stay consistent.

Core Takeaway: Your Journey, Your Legacy

Celebrating your unique humanity isn't about chasing perfection—it's about living authentically, sharing your strengths, and embracing life's journey with intention and confidence.

Every step you take, whether big or small, contributes to a legacy of authenticity, compassion, and growth. By honoring your individuality and sharing your gifts, you create a brighter future for yourself and those around you.

Let this chapter serve as a powerful reminder: your individuality is your greatest asset. Embrace it, celebrate it, and let the world witness your authentic brilliance.

Step forward boldly—the world is waiting to celebrate you.

THAT'S A WRAP!

FINAL THOUGHTS

Step Forward with Human Pride and Purpose

Take a deep breath and savor this moment. You've done something extraordinary—not just finishing a book but choosing to invest in yourself, your growth, and your potential. This was more than reading; it was an act of courage and commitment. Every reflection, every insight, and every step forward has brought you closer to celebrating the remarkable person you are.

But this isn't the end of your journey. It's the beginning. You now stand at the threshold of a new chapter, equipped with the tools and inspiration to create a life of purpose, connection, and fulfillment.

ANCHORING IN HUMAN PRIDE

Human pride is a profound acknowledgment of your inherent worth. It's about living authentically, leading with empathy, and embracing your ability to make a difference.

Human pride is a profound acknowledgment of your inherent worth

255

- **Authenticity** allows you to show up as your full self—your strengths, vulnerabilities, and quirks—and creates spaces of trust and connection. This quiet but powerful form of leadership starts with self-acceptance and radiates outward, inspiring others to do the same.
- **Empowerment** is the ripple effect of your actions. Each time you encourage, support, or celebrate someone else, you leave a lasting impact. Carry this spirit forward, knowing your small acts of kindness contribute to a world where everyone feels capable of achieving their potential.

THE RELATIONSHIPS THAT DEFINE US

At its core, human pride thrives on connection. Think about the relationships that have shaped your life—moments of shared laughter, vulnerability, and understanding. These connections are the threads of your story.

Make it your mission to deepen these bonds and create new ones. Each interaction is an opportunity to inspire, mentor, and listen with intention. The ripple effect of a single genuine moment can transform lives, including your own.

LIVING YOUR LEGACY

Your legacy isn't something distant; it's what you create every single day. It's in the words you speak, the choices you make, and the way you show up for others and yourself.

Ask yourself:

- What do I want my legacy to be?

- How can I empower others or bring light into the world?
- What values will guide me as I build this legacy?

Remember, your legacy is unfolding right now—one thoughtful, intentional act at a time.

A COMMITMENT TO LIFELONG GROWTH

Growth is a journey, not a destination. It requires courage to face uncertainty, adapt to change, and celebrate progress—even when it feels small. As you move forward, make room for reflection and self-compassion. Honor your struggles, celebrate your victories, and remain curious about what's possible.

Trust in your ability to navigate life's complexities, knowing every experience adds depth and resilience to your journey.

FINAL REFLECTIONS

Before you close this book, take a moment to reflect on what you've learned and how it will shape your future.

1. **What have you discovered about yourself?** Reflect on the insights you've gained and the strengths you've uncovered. How will you use these lessons to live with greater intention and purpose?
2. **What legacy do you want to build?** Envision the impact you want to have on the people and communities around you. What steps can you take today to start creating that legacy?
3. **How will you celebrate your humanity?** Embrace the qualities that make you unique. How can you honor and share those gifts with the world?

THE JOURNEY CONTINUES

As you close this chapter, step boldly into the future, guided by human pride, fueled by authenticity, and inspired by connection.

Your voice, your actions, and your humanity have the power to create ripples far beyond what you can see. The world needs your courage, your kindness, and your authenticity.

Move forward with intention.

Move forward with courage.

Move forward with human pride.

With love and gratitude,

Ron